Nineteen
Lines:
A
Drawing
Center
Writing
Anthology

Nineteen Lines: A Drawing Center Writing Anthology

Edited by
Lytle Shaw

ROOF BOOKS
NEW YORK

The Drawing Center

ISBN 10: 1-931824-25-8
ISBN 13: 978-1-931824-25-5
Library of Congress Control Number: 2007924250

Roof Books are published by
The Segue Foundation
300 Bowery
New York, NY 10012
seguefoundation.com

Roof Books are distributed by
Small Press Distribution
1341 Seventh Avenue
Berkeley, CA 94710-1403
Phone orders: 800-869-7553
spdbooks.org

 This book was made possible, in part, with public funds from the New York State Council on the Arts, a state agency.

NYSCA

The Drawing Center
35 Wooster Street
New York, NY 10013
drawingcenter.org

Drawing Center Publications
Adam Lehner, *Executive Editor*
Joanna Berman, *Managing Editor*
Kavior Moon, *Publications Assistant*

Designed by Peter J. Ahlberg

The Drawing Center's 2006–2007 publications are made possible, in part, through a contribution to the Edward Hallam Tuck Publication Program from The Felix and Elizabeth Rohatyn Foundation, Inc.

Edward Hallam Tuck Publication Program

CONTENTS

PREFACE

In presenting the Line Reading series, The Drawing Center sought to combine its exhibition program with a literary program investigating the extent to which the boundaries between the fields of literature and visual art can be crossed. Promoting the dialogue between contemporary writing and drawing, Line Readings featured writers whose works provided a context for this interaction. The majority of the texts included here are by emerging, New York–based writers who were selected both for their cutting-edge work in poetry and prose and for the links in their writing to the drawings on display in The Drawing Center's spaces. For art audiences, Line Readings expanded awareness of contemporary pioneering writers. For authors, they brought greater exposure and an opportunity for direct contact with new audiences. In Lytle Shaw, The Drawing Center was fortunate to have such a zealous curator of the series: an Assistant Professor of English at New York University, he is himself an accomplished poet and critic and the co-editor of *Shark*, a journal of poetics and art writing. From 2000 to 2002, Lytle invited over fifty writers, poets, and book artists to participate in the Line Readings, all of whom are included in this excellent anthology.

The Line Reading series continued The Drawing Center's tradition of exploring correlations between the literary and the drawn, evident in such exhibitions as *Shadows of the Hand: The Drawings of Victor Hugo* (1998), *Untitled Passages by Henri Michaux* (2000), *Korwa Drawings: Contemporary Tribal Works on Paper from Central India* (2000), and in the work of contemporary artist Adrianne Gallinari (2001). Viewing work by artist-writers such as Victor Hugo (1802–1885) and Henri Michaux (1899–1984), both of whom worked within a spectrum that ranged from the merely visible to the highly legible, one could argue that drawing and writing follow the same logic of creativity and desire in the inscriptive gesture of tracing. They share a process that is, above all, about the hand exploring a given space, traveling over paper, and organizing it according to its own possibilities. The tracing process, as it follows the line of thought to which it gives form, can be considered a practice forever on the point of drifting off course. In writing, according to Martine Reid, "this appears during the pauses and hesitations of the thought process, when the pen can be caught accomplishing other gestures: additions, scribbles, and the excessive embellishment of letters, the transformation of words, lines, and inkblots into heads, animals, or other, less creditable things—'the hand talks' says Dubuffet. The visible returns and jostles with the legible: it is unpretentious, playful, useless, and it draws writing towards making." Unfolding both the visual and the written expression of marks made on the blank page, The Drawing Center attempted to present, analyze, and experiment with—to open—our conception of the possibilities that exist beyond the conventions of the graphic/drawn sign.

Few are more conscious and eloquent than Michaux about the relationship between the written text and drawing, writing's liberating counterpart. Insofar as Michaux considers drawing as a discourse of enactment and writing as a discourse of knowledge, his position can be compared to what Giorgio Agamben describes in Western culture as the fundamental scission of the world, the notion "that poetry possesses its object without knowing it while philosophy knows its object without possessing it. The word is thus divided between a word that is unaware, as if fallen from the sky, and enjoys the object of knowledge by representing it in beautiful form, and a word that has all seriousness and consciousness for itself but does not enjoy its object because it does not know how to represent it." However, Michaux, who was fascinated by non-rational experiences and non-Western traditions, tried again and again to upset the old imperatives of differentiation between drawing and writing by developing a continuous exchange. "The genesis of the text, as of any written mark (particularly that of drawing), must be considered from the viewpoint of the original spatial play which the hand stages. Neither the paradigm of the eye nor that of language allows us to grasp the meaning of 'first draft' dynamics—the moment when its enunciation is born in distinction from what it enunciates. The paradigm of the hand, however, achieves such an understanding. Originally what is at stake in the hand is the very nature of the psychic investments which are bound up in it."

—Catherine de Zegher
Executive Director, The Drawing Center (1999–2006)

INTRODUCTION

Since its beginning in April 2000, the Line Reading series put contemporary innovative writers in dialogue with The Drawing Center's exhibitions.
Often this meant concrete, causal links between the two media: writers who
were influenced by or collaborated with artists. But for the many exhibitions
whose connections to literature were less direct, the series also attempted,
provisionally and by different means each time, to suggest how terms crucial
to an artist or artistic movements might find analogs within contemporary
writing. Thus the introductions stress those features of a poet's work that
speak both to the general art and poetry context of the series and to the
specific occasion of each exhibition. This self-imposed constraint at the
base of the Line Reading series made it necessary for me both to skip over
or condense significant aspects of each poet's work and also to pursue
interdisciplinary links that emerged in part from the possibility of placing
the two art forms together. But if this constraint heightened the partiality
and contingency fundamental to the genre of the reading introduction, it
also allowed for recent poetry to be framed both within broader spheres of
contemporary culture (from which it is too often excluded) and within the
historical dialogue between art and poetry.

Obviously there is a long tradition of such dialogue and collaboration in
New York City. Its recent chapters, however, remain affected by the separate
economic and institutional conditions that drove the two arts apart in the
1980s. That many younger artists look, for instance, to the poetry of the
1950s for their inspiration, rather than to their contemporaries, suggests
the extent to which recent poetry is either ignored or misunderstood. The
problem is not simply one of its "difficulty." While within art, the theoretical and social turn in the 1970s and 1980s was well documented and widely
discussed, this is less the case with contemporary poetry. Despite poets'
frequent and various attempts to situate their projects within social and
intellectual history, despite the vast and articulate writings of experimental-
ists from the Objectivists to the Black Mountain, San Francisco Renaissance,
New York School, Language, and Post-Language poets, poetry as a whole
is often still taken as a solidly autobiographical discourse concerned either
with confession or with private experience. A central goal of the series,
then, was to display contemporary poetry as it extends into, and engages

with, other scales than that of the private "I" (from the intersubjective to the collective, the urban, and even the global) and other domains of inquiry other than the I's interior (from philosophy and social theory to linguistics, performance, and sound art) to name just a few of the areas within which some of the writers included here stage their work.

—Lytle Shaw

The Prinzhorn Collection: Traces upon the Wunderblock

April 18, 2000

Brian Kim Stefans
Kenward Elmslie
Bernadette Mayer

The artists of the Prinzhorn Collection, named after the German art historian and psychiatrist, Hans Prinzhorn, who amassed the works, were patients in European psychiatric hospitals from about 1890 to 1920. Their drawings have been an object of intense fascination for members of the European avant-garde (including the Surrealists, Jean Dubuffet, and Max Ernst) eager to identify themselves with marginality and a would-be liberating concept of un-reason. One of the occasions provided by this exhibition is thus to think about the functions that identification with unreason and marginality have historically performed for artists and for culture more broadly. These functions have clearly shifted between the Europe of 1920 and the United States of 2000: there are now few critics, for instance, who still take poetry as a truly marginal, authentic practice of unreason. Rather than demonstrate how poetry's "unreason" disrupts normative regimes of meaning and socialization, it seems far more relevant now to suggest how poetry, in its very semantic multiplicity, produces exemplary models for the making of complex, and therefore useful, meanings. Which is not to say that poets generally, and the poets in the first reading in particular—Brian Kim Stefans, Kenward Elmslie, Bernadette Mayer—are no longer concerned with challenging normative notions of rationality, only that this no longer happens through an identification with madness, and that fascination with a failure to make sense now seems to have been superseded by the desire to proliferate senses.

The overloaded, exuberant referentiality of Brian Kim Stefans's lines offer one version of this proliferation. At home equally with Gerard Manley Hopkins and Brian Eno, Stefans's rapidly moving poems inventively mine the history of literature and popular culture for troubling and rich raw material. Brought to a special kind of un-light through vertiginous substitutions and qualifications, the poems refuse to cash in on this material, to convert it into the basis of a secure subject position or identity. Instead, Stefans takes on a funny and irreverent exploration of the conventional bases of identities, and of their relations to institutional power. In A Poem of Attitudes, for instance, he uses the would-be neutral rationality of computerized alphabetization programs to organize the recalcitrant psychic matter contained in spontaneously composed sentences. Within the ambient landscape of the alphabetized phrases, Stefans's own sentences also merge with a wide range of found materials—poetry quotations, pop-music reviews, literary criticism.

Kenward Elmslie's works engage many of the textual and visual terms of Dadaism, Surrealism, and Pop Art in an utterly homemade, quirky context often characterized by humorous linguistic density. Building mosaics from equal part 1940s Broadway

show tune, pureed anthropological field report, and scandalous high-culture aside,
Elmslie's writing projects an impossibly composite speaker as it wanders between lin-
guistically experimental poetry and ambitious deformations of popular music, between
dense poetic stanzas and deceptively neat iconic images (often provided by his longtime
partner, the late artist Joe Brainard, with whom Elmslie frequently collaborated).

In the late 1960s, Bernadette Mayer co-edited the journal 0 to 9 *with the artist Vito*
Acconci. While Acconci was turning his body into a site of experimentation, Mayer
was developing modes of serial, project-based poetry that organized mass aggregates of
experience through the trope of the assignment or the self-imposed research project—all
that could be remembered about a month of experience using only photographs or
everything that could be compiled in relation to topics like utopias or movement. Some
of the books of the 1970s and early 1980s that came out of this approach include
Memory, Moving, Studying Hunger, Utopia, *and* Midwinter Day. *Far from*
bureaucratic or scientistic, however, Mayer's poetry unhinges the research project from
its secure disciplinary backing, reimagining the unbounded potential of inquiry and
enumeration as forms of disruptive and uncontainable pleasure. In doing this Mayer
moves freely among both poetic and non-poetic genres—from field notes and treatises to
sonnets, epics, and journals. —LS

Brian Kim Stefans
from *A Poem of Attitudes*

Distances
measured in hype-years. Distracting.
Dithering off.
Dizzyingly, futzing
sanity, not bump the borders, the theory
being that. Do no matter. No noise of
walking. No, they smell spam
in the hamptons.
Other pasty faces lathering the windows.
No pop.
No rain fell for the emperor
tching tang, grain scarce. No yes. No.

See that nasty graffiti. Seeing there's
seven pianos, like a constable
in
the warp. Stares. Select output. Thereby
affecting the whole living lack of
courage
theretofore. And the mercantilism of
neo-logs cure. These are brake fluids
—her bowels contracted and the cautious
entry into the corridors of art. And
sex and logic are
criteria or criminals.
Sexual acts and the kitschy applauses
one stacks the nations singular corpse.
And the other blokes from hitchcock's
theatre

sexual preferences

in graphic,

an epic sphere. Her gait is dull. Her

    hand on shelves. These detail. Shadows

        on the sands of tranquility phase court

   where earlier had been the demonstration

against the academy no one demeaned.

        Shaker ethics—and the penis it creates.

        And the prince-esque nicotine and gravy.

And then wimps

out. And then your example

    of the bricks born that devolve

all baroque intentions

 into the

again.

       These eddies of thought not contagious?

  These knees. These screens are image,

image is color. Of the earth. She's also

      a bibliophile. She absently pisan cantos.

      And they revel in the steamy sonics

of the sb-jam. And thought: we wonder

     greets

    with an affected. She approaches

from the poised tremulously. Her name

was theresa. Herbie

  distant fleck but

  fleck of something

  to bargain with.

      These statements are only provisional

  they say. Video with a these trysts

of banging heads that smother. These

  virginal submissions, slight groan.

  She desists. She entered.

    She intrudes. She

  intrudes. She lived—are really resubmissions.

They're collecting them of the "vaginal
        pastoral." And we wonder who wore the
                trinket in a book by
anon. As a cheap
chain round his gat through the war.

As a person he was chaos for dips, intent
                on the merely puerile or charming. As
        are my hopes. As factual as arithmetic
curses for cities. As I'm doing now.

And by waking
        be them: a leather jellyfish
dying in
the sun. And cursors. And dissimilar.
                And forget about the whole rotten country,
                it's a skitterbug. And forgets
        managed
        to remain in the news: he felt. He knocks
                my lemonade. And he eventually married
        as many as 19, sleeps in spurs
knowledge, the shirt unbuttoned. The
        sloth. The snaps different quarters.
                Rather. Rather. Rather. Recall soulsonic
        cult women, and fathered
at least 10 of their tap.
                The stalker vase of poinsettias
        into hell. Erodes over
        the mound horizon.
                The force. Recordings. Records
        of stamping of ants. The stardust
                munchkins: he measured the length of
        syntax
        of the tubes to children. And
in her eyeballs motion him to the buffet

table where they entreat
vengeance were
             a toss to treaties, redolent. Reefs.
Draped with sinewy lashes. And in this
him to vote
for them. The strategy of
             the left-off:
Reelect these boundaries.
Relax.
Remarkable—Renan. Report switch
make tune for song
twenty-six (that
             was) and 25 code. Retreat into the populated
pallid males of his making, his
      tomb
      is today in extras.

      Revelers
   in cities, this was in
the twenty fifth century.
      He never
   was able
   to supply and demand of
             the subaltern: the still unmixed
   sweet and flux
of encouragements, idiolect's
temperaments. Mailed sleeve surface is
             not enough. The sweet were
      never so
      low
produces the new musical category
   and musk satellites quiver in the
             mesh of these fancily
             prettified selves,

such fear in the debutante heart. Rex's
zip,
spastic
future funk. And more. And
    obtuse. And old school jams. And other
        talk-songs: gun, boogie. Rice. Rickets
    of prose. Rickets. Of curiosity. And
pile atop the mounds
    of cuss
        erecting, roar like
        the laundry swirl
    neat as on my typewriter.
He put, speaking their
    customs in the dark. The traffic slick.

Kenward Elmslie

No Liquor in the House

1.
Lizzie Murder Music included,
cue accident. Loose teeth

(long run) unaffordable.
Affable Ishy, handsome rambler.

Despite familial dread (plot),
stuck with bus & burb Macheath.

Prissy? He clarifies *butter!*
Death Breath time scrambler

2.
proffers could Dutch lips.
Yet another kiss from Youth Hell.

Need my zzzzzs, so nibble mesclun,
wolf Cherry Garcia.

Arrogant prick! I mutter-mutter
hot threat. Move O-U-T. Hotel.

Rewrites? *Quel horreur!*
Gee, I once went to a Dr. Swee. A-

3.

squat, Jack Beeson, as if homeless, snacked,
seersucker impeccable, on the sidewalk,

pre-gig. Coffee-cig truce. Philip Roth
(breakthrough—"civilized" discourse)

now a recluse. Helen of Troy
sashay is how *I'd walk*

through killing fields, back to
boyhood, Blue Nile source.

Bernadette Mayer
from *Spring Journal, 2000*

march 20, 2000
when i saw the first coltsfoot blossoming on the first day of spring i
realized that spring 2000 had to be kept track of, plus i like saying
spring 2000.

march 25, 00
we heard peepers today, first time this year, we being me, max, alissa
and phil. i ate a flower at the blue plate restaurant, a dandelion-like
thing. there are coltsfoot everywhere, shared a snapdragon with alissa.

april 14, 00
saw a bear last night. saw trout lilies growing on the banks of the tsat-
sawassa creek. we showed grace and maeve the house and bodies of
water and finished emptying the van of the stuff from storage.

april 20, 00
being in new orleans is like being in an octagonal house. last night
we saw bo diddley at the house of blues. we got tickets thru dave from
a guy named lucky who supervises the kitchen there. here we are tour-
ists, we went thru the french market. we even bought post-cards and
one has a lobster on it, got a voodoo doll for our hosts. dave has an
impeccable library. he even has a copy of the anecdoted typography
of chance

april 24, 00
lafayette, louisiana. my allergies are so bad i can see herons and
horses that eat apples all the time. we went to dave's mother's house
where we saw deer, goats, chickens, eloquent snakes, you are eminent-
ly replaceable. we went to avery island and saw a whole slew of egrets.
we ate mountains of crawfish. went to prejean's (me, phil, jerry, skip,
mac and kyle).

april 28, 00
outside agitators were we in pensacola. we saw a lot of people picking up their welfare checks all dated "the egg, albany, new york." of
an ocean or in this case the gulf of mexico, you can only see a part. i
have some magnolia blossoms.

april 30 monday
another stunning frost, cant plant anything but peas & spinach,
there's so much to do today before our journey to new orleans i think
i'll either make a list or go back to bed. the ravens are at the birdfeeder, & so is a squirrel, it must be a desperately cold morning. got the
recipe for dandelion wine, the ravens look awkward. i feel as awkward
as a raven at a birdfeeder, the finches, on the other hand, are elegant
& it's frozen still, harking fairly forward. pileated woodpecker reflects
the sun.
        dream i am ate a poetry gathering & find a hidden bathroom
you enter by a mirror with an arctic diorama in front of it. "who's in
there?" i ask. "it's 3-tinkle maurice" i'm told (maurice kenny). then
traveling around, i see the perfect maroon lounge chair (the uphol-
stered kind) at a used furniture sale for $40. but we can't figure out
how to get it back to east nassau. so i came back without it both in
conscious life and elsewhere, so much for dreams.
today i have to pick dandelion greens to freeze, then pack my bag, for
some reason i keep wanting to say 'ha ha,' sorry.

april 31
no frost (?) disorganization total, who cares?
/ ; 1/2 @#$% ^&*; oops whoa ziggurat hymnal wherefore impetus
shower.

may 10
back to here. leaves & dandelions, wasps in beer. last night impressive
moon. i dreamt the question ' would you be willing to be a heretic'
and apparently i answered when phil entered the room, i don't know
the answer to that question, but i didn't know what the question was,

it was a confusing day. however i began to make dandelion wine for the first time, i picked all the dandelions and will now heat sugar in water, what happens later i will not relate, let us hope it will taste ok. it's a weird world we live in but at least every spring so far dandelions have arisen. they are in abundance here and i'll do the next step of wine-making now.

may 11

there are so many things undone they'll probably remain that way, i give up except i'll plant the wildflower seeds & go thru the motions of celebrating my birthday, & then we'll continue in this fucked up way, who cares? phil always angry, doing things separately, i'm learning to play that game and this is not a game you play competitively, or at least i don't know how…after all i'm not a masochist in that way. who cares? even to put the question mark in the place it goes.

may 12

something about the (avens?) group of lily. that's all i know.

may 13

some dandelions have become puffballs while i was celebrating my birthday, there's an elephant in a birdbath in my field of vision. i know there's a turtle in the garden—misting turtle. & a raven at the bird feeder. we had an awe-inspiring time at bartholomew's cobble with sophie & zac yesterday and then ate, freezing, outdoors and hudson's where i had duck & pistachio pate, creamed spinach with pernod, potato & cheese balls, death by chocolate, a langavalin & much fresh mint & dill. i also got to taste everything else. now i'm imbibing cranberry juice on a cool cloudy mother's day during which there is much to do but i won't do any of it except pick lilacs at the abandoned house up the road & sleep & dream. i don't think i will even look for anything but find things. it is definitely a columbine day & here come the bluejays. nobody appeared last night, but a chipmunk.

may 14

i have so not begun to relate the half of it i don't know how to start. it looks like there's a frost this morning but that would be breaking all the rules since the full moon of may is over. mother nature an anarchist: I'm always looking for a reason to go back to bed but this is the best ever. the most recent thing i can't find is my friederike mayröcker book, it's almost as cold as a witch's tit out here. a bluejay is taking a bath, well a drink. magic hat magic hat.

may 15

i had such a weird nightmare yesterday i couldn't even speak about it & i'm hoping by doing that now i'll annihilate its effect. i was telling phil i wanted him to be sane not crazy and then i was about to get shot…

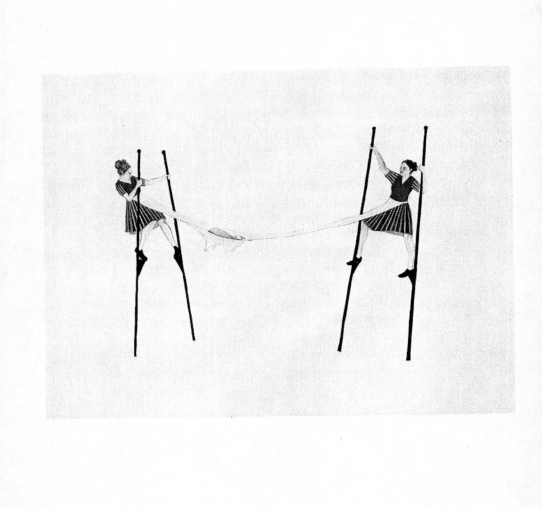

Selections Summer 2000

June 21, 2000

Dan Farrell
Carla Harryman

Unlike the first reading, which was organized in direct response to the drawings of the Prinzhorn Collection, the second reading occurred during the non-thematic Selections Summer 2000 *exhibition. Rather than try to explore parallels between the drawings and the poetry, this reading presented recent innovative writing that runs against two of the dominant features of recent experimental poetry: an emphasis on the line as poetry's fundamental unit, and the practice of line-to-line disjunctions in meaning.*

One of the ways that recent poetry has sought to describe or enact consciousness, and especially consciousness in a social world, is by activating gaps in meaning between lines, to proliferate references and destabilize referents. According to this model of the disjunctive text, if one resists sequential narration and consistent referentiality, writing may begin to enact, and not merely describe, social space. Compared to much recent poetry, then, Dan Farrell's recent work is not disjunctive. While the unfolding sentences do not resolve into a consistent logical position, or even into a consistent "I," neither do they wander freely among discourses. Instead Farrell proposes both a consistent framing and a narrowing of referentiality that connect his work to models of institutional critique explored by recent art. One of his sites of inquiry—developed in a piece like "Avail" from his 1999 book Last Instance *and throughout his forthcoming* The Inkblot Record—*has been the way that the psychological wing of the medical industry talks to itself and to others. Rather than simply point out contradictions or mistakes in an act of negation, Farrell has invented a way of thinking simultaneously inside and outside of medicine, pointing inventively to frames and presuppositions that structure and guide thought there, while staging a refusal to be guided. This refusal occurs not by imagining an integral and whole self prior to all forms of measurement, but instead by tracking the self to the zones of its fascinating illegibility as it gets constituted in the specific regimes of medical description. This tracking happens in* The Inkblot Record *by probing the epistemological underpinnings of the Rorschach Test, a test that bears a particularly important relation to poets insofar as it proposes to read a fixed set of psychological "profiles" out of the analogies—the figurative associations—a patient uses to describe abstract shapes. Farrell's text also presents a model of language being directed at abstract visual experience—a continuous scene of visual interpretation that itself gives rise, in the structure of the Rorschach test, to a symptomatic reading of the first reading.*

Since the late 1970s, Carla Harryman has been one of the most inventive prose writers in the poetry world. Like Dan Farrell, she eschews a certain kind of familiar disjunc-

tion at the level of the clause in order to develop larger conceptual disjunctions, ones that also can be seen in institutional terms—not merely institutions like narrative (with the world its causal chains project), but also the more unspoken institutional pressures that keep disciplines in their places, literature being literature, philosophy philosophy, witchcraft witchcraft, et cetera. What separates Harryman's work from a great deal of writing also proposing interdisciplinarity is that hers is less a plea for some future state than an example in operation. While only some of Harryman's writing is dramatic, her work is a continuous acting out—both in the common senses implied above and in the less common sense she has invented for literature of giving a kind of embodiment, and even volition or consciousness, to ideas. This used to be called allegory; but certainly the eighteenth-century version would not recognize itself (or its moral ambitions) in the odd and shifting costumes Harryman proposes for it. Instead, one might say that what gets acted out, and reinvented, are the rhetorical and narrative raw materials from which truth effects have been built in literature and social life more generally. —LS

Dan Farrell

from *The Inkblot Record*

I didn't say that, I said a crab with wings, these are the wings, it's a
crab, that's all. I didn't say that, you wrote it wrong, it's a whale and
see his face there, here's his nose and his chin and his big long body
like a whale. I didn't see faces. I don't get much from the white thing,
but if I just use this darker part it looks like two dogs rubbing noses. I
don't get much out of this one except, you know, this middle red part
could be like a clown's mouth, the lips, I'm not sure if you know what
I mean, but it could be like you might paint human lips to exagger-
ate them, that's all though. I don't get too much more out of this one
unless it could be a bee too. I don't know. I don't know. I don't know.
I don't know. I don't know anything else that comes out of a bottle.
I don't know—bitter beetles. I don't know, it looks like some kind of
leg like of a person with the toes curled up. I don't know, just a lot
of garbage I guess, it doesn't make much sense to me. I don't know,
just somebody funny. I don't know, maybe it's a flying squirrel, what
do most people see in these things? I don't know much about them,
this one is weird 'cause it's got this pointy thing coming out the top,
like a stinger, see up here and the rest of it is white like some kind
of weird insect. I don't know of any butterflies that go from brown
to old rose, butterfly has no head. I don't know the name, it has a
special name. I don't know what it's going through, just stuff but it's
coming out this side, you can see the path it took, it looks like that
to me. I don't know what made me say that. I don't know what made
me think of that, I suppose the arch effect, like a cartoon character,
when the bowleggedness is over-emphasized like this, you see this is
the trunk and these are the skinny legs, they take this stance sometimes. I don't know what made me think of that, maybe I'm hungry,
it's just all red like ketchup but you sure don't put it on stone crab.
I don't know what the heck they are. I don't know which countries
these could be. I don't know why badgers are climbing on it. I don't
know why I see Scotties, I don't like them. I don't know why I thought
of channel. I don't know why she swallowed the fly, perhaps she'll die.
I don't like arguments. I don't like it. I don't like them. I don't like
this either, there's another butterfly down here, like getting ready to

land on this black part. I don't like this one, it looks like a dead cat. I don't mean his sex but his sign, the ones that are hung (giggles) on his shop to let people know what he is, he'll lend you money and things. I don't remember that, I think it must be here a red one, you can see the large leaves. I don't remember what kind of butterfly it is that has large circles on its back, like eyes, makes birds think it's eyes to frighten them off. I don't remember what you call them, gyplane or something, you wrap a string on them and pull and they balance like this for a long time. I don't see anything else though. I don't see it end, it might be any length. I don't see nothin' else there. I don't see the holes for the eyes but the form is right for one. I don't think anything about what I see. I don't think he ever reached it. I don't think I was right. I don't think of them as a teamwork, you know? I don't understand him anymore, he doesn't show things like he used to, he talks about very intellectual things. I feel as if it keeps waving this things, these two winglike arms, helplessly, but it wouldn't do any good. I feel like—I used to feel stronger in my idealism than right now. I feel like I'm a very bitter person, the square butterfly looks like a bitter butterfly. I feel like it could be disintegrated or blown away. I felt it was phony. I felt it was very humiliating. I get a general impression of all kinds of squirmy animals. I get the impression of something from Greek mythology, like a woman standing there, like a goddess with smoke or fog on each side, that's all I see. I get the impression of two animals like billy goats or deer butting their heads, like they do in a mating struggle. I got a beating for it, I was jealous of the cat getting more attention than I did. I got a feeling of feet upright. I guess he's not very friendly, if someone took his head off. I guess I'd say a hawk, see the big wings and these here are the feet that can grab things easy when they are out looking for prey, they have these really sharp claws. I guess it could also be an insect, has claws to grab. I guess it could be a couple of African women pulling an animal apart. I guess it could be a wolf kinda growling. I guess it's an island and this part is like a harbor, you know. I guess it's supposed to be a symbol of strength, but not for me, are fearful, ruthless birds. I guess I've been playing Dungeons and Dragons too long. I guess the square of 'em with rough edges. I guess this center part could be a crab or something like a crab. I guess underneath the gray birds' legs, looks like eyes, V, like camel's face with V being nose. I guess you could call it that. I had earaches, eye infections. I had strange communications with him, I thought he was diabolical. I hated that cat, I tried to flush him down the toilet, I once threw him out a four-story window, he landed on someone's face, and the guy came up to our apartment all bloody. I have a tendency to think I'll get—I'll always end up with the short end of the stick. I heard somewhere if you see that stuff you're preoccupied with it, is that right? I held the card right side up. I hope not, no one should see that, it's the huge thing here and the rest is her. I just can't say, it's too awful. I just generally think of the story, they were OK because they were passed over. I just get the feeling from this part. I just had a funny thought. I just inferred it. I just respond in terms of a touching quality. I just see the head; he is puffing hard on the cigarette. I know I should try to make something of it. I know what that looks like. I like flowers and I see some tulips here, yellow tulips. I like it better like this, now that's a bird, like an eagle zooming up. I like this color, there's a map there, like islands. I mean explosion, I never heard of a implosion, I mean explosion, see, like it's all going up (gestures with hands) and this orange is like the fire part when that happens, I didn't say implosion though, explosion, that's what I said.

Carla Harryman
from *The Words after Carl Sandburg's Rootabaga Stories
and Jean-Paul Sartre*

Expansion

Woemess baked in the sad plains. She was as unreal as a discovery
made elsewhere.

"During the entombment there were others like me. We read a
lot, under the common eyes of sight of every woman. But only that
which has no history can be defined. I, myself, am the consequence of
a barbaric union and utopian vision or barbaric and utopian vision or
barbaric and utopian union, a marriage or plan, an instinct or idea. I
was taught that I was already living in paradise and, therefore, had no
need to represent it in the imagination.

"Then the word barbaric and the knowledge of barbarism became a form of deception in history; thus, something that could not
be described.

"And I wondered while others wondered too, what happened to
our celebration as if loss had replaced description? Is what we carry
with ourselves of the barbaric, now annulled, that interstitial flux that
has woken me, my words, unstrung without a purse to hold them?
Oh, but my mind wanders.

"I lived where I died with the Utopians packaging their books in
trompe l'oeil boxes, taken to a jail that no longer functioned as a jail.
The Utopians fought their enemies by confounding them, by turning
old news into new news by turning gossip into aborted anecdotes and
religious treatises. Utopia lasted for a long time and fell apart. The
books were taken out, put back in their trick containers, taken out,
etc. It was a great joy for all those who had no sense of local history to
play there. The ecstatic state was never entirely abandoned, but more
of a mood that came and went. Events came and went, were parasiti-
cal on play, and could never be fully assigned to the effects of culture.
It was not a culture that added up. Its mathematics were so complex
that people, when they encountered numbers, often fell into trances;
therefore, it took a very long time to accomplish mundane things.
Some say that all of us were sacrificed because of the mass psyche. But

who could track the mass psyche in a culture that didn't add up? I would like to challenge the mass psyche theorists, first, to say the word *woman*.

"When we ask," she continued while fanning a curl inside the bleakest alcove of her cogito in order to reform it, "if I speak will my mood change, we celebrate a fragmentary appreciation of the effect of genre fiction.

"One day, I was laying on a pink-laden mat in the prison with my cohort, Svelta. I was making the observation that non-fiction and fiction had become the same thing. For instance, I said to her, just think of how many times *once upon a time* has appeared recently in both juridical papers and art historical documents. Svelta, an extraordinarily well-educated person, would have none of this discussion. We went into the street, like you Stranded, and slept.

Woemess took a pack of cards from a pocket stitched to the inside of her dangerous-looking apron. She turned the first four cards over, face up. They read:

denotation, setting, eroticism, projection

"If one wants to continue to breathe in the sweet salt air, one has to admit that it is there."

She put the first three cards in her mouth and chewed for a very long time. After a while, she picked up the last card, labeled *projection*, and fiddled with it. Finally, she spit out the wad of other cards and tossed them into a nearby landscape. She flapped her apron, creating a stirring wind around her as if she had just risen from the dead.

And thus her speech continued.

"High on a hill is a lascivious dictator. He grunts with phallic exuberance and hairy tits into the ditch of his pledges. The pledges zoom over the surface of the ditch when he tickles them. They bite his tongue in playful nips and unzip the hairs on the nape of his neck whenever he says the word ooh in imitation of entombed women. This is why, when he speaks, everybody wants to return to the body of their mothers and stops working. When he sees his subjects wandering in the forest among the white cedars flecked by sunlight and open wind, he nabs them. Jealous of their desires, he extracts their death drives with splendid whips, sticks, and metal bars that shine with the passions of all those they have touched. When the bad guy dictator rubs his hands over the weapons rununculus petals, which smell like dogs breath when bled on, cling to the skin of each of those he's nabbed. As if they were inking newspapers, other rancid flowers drop out of the hands of passersby onto his bare toes, while the nihilist, to whom I was betrothed before the decision to sacrifice me had been made, prods his erect cock with jokes he's brought back from another world. In this everlasting silence of sheen and scars, the dictator and the nihilist pause at irregular intervals to relish the noise of scratching under the baseboards of the lascivious dictator's rotund habitation.

"I suppose you would like to hear a little more about his method of governance."

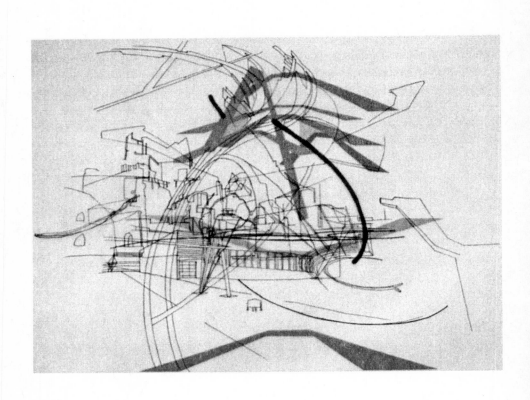

Selections Fall 2000

September 12, 2000

Marcella Durand
Lewis Warsh
Lynne Tillman

While this exhibition was officially non-thematic, it was often discussed informally in terms of architecture. For many of the artists included, architecture is an occasion to invent fragmentary narrative forms (based on superimpositions and juxtapositions) in which different representational modes complicate and expand each other: in Grady Gerbracht's work, it's the sketch and the urban landscape as seen through a bus window for an instant; in Julie Mehretu's work, the perspectival rendering of architectural spaces along with the dots, stains, and squiggles of a two-dimensional spatial order; in Geraldine Lau's wall piece, the lines of imagined communication or trade paths among island nations as well as systems of pins that suggest population or building density. If to provide such a description is already to imagine temporal sequences (and figurative associations) that extend from the frozen moment of each artwork, these artists' use of architectural and cartographic conventions tends to encourage this sort of part-by-part interpretation. The work is in this sense narrative, and architectural, without always looking like buildings or building toward narrative conclusions. Like the Selections artists, the three writers reading have labored to reformulate the problems of sequence and narrative within their writing. All have, in different ways, moreover, understood the literary as a way to trace how we read the visual world—be it charting the massive material movements flowing in and out of New York, the flow of cultural capital and ideology through museums, or the bodily apparatuses that would register such phenomena in the first place.

The poet Marcella Durand does not write narrative per se; she composes collections of linked poems, like her City of Ports, a serial book whose accumulating urban details map both the flows of substance through "the city"—New York and equally an "unbuildable city" of the imagination—and the more static systems (from construction techniques to economics) that allow for this movement. Ports, here, are not only nautical, but also all portals—electronic, bodily, architectural. The density and multiple inflections of her poetic language figure the coincidence of materials and the systems that underlie them. But rather than fix these in finalized images, Durand's poetry uses its serial, sequential approach to build in a form of re-seeing and consequent rethinking, which is, after all, fundamental to quotidian urban experience. That her exuberant results do not depend upon a familiar metaphysics of unity ("I am one with the city," or "The city is one") allows her cartographic project to extend its relevance beyond the small intellectual cartouche often reserved for poetic speculations about urbanism.

In the 1970s, Lewis Warsh began to experiment with a kind of encyclopedic poetry that accumulated detail in an almost narrative way. The four sections of Methods of Birth Control, *for instance, examine sight, reproductive genes, hearing, and birth control. There are tonal shifts and carefully placed contradictions that disrupt the seamless dispensing of "fact"; nevertheless, it is a poetry of learning about quotidian objects in real time (like the bees of his 1979 book* Hives) *without the pretense of "poetic language." In more recent poems and fiction, this almost minimalist exploration expands, or returns, into first person experience and fictional relationships: here, however, character tends to glide outside itself. In his novel* Agnes & Sally, *for instance, this happens formally, with one story getting framed and reframed by a footnote text that emerges periodically. In the poems, this displacement happens thematically, as the focus shifts into the history of objects, social practices, and other consciousnesses that enter for very short periods of time. The result, throughout, is a practice that invents new portals among poetry, fiction and autobiography.*

Lynne Tillman's Madame Realism, of the book bearing her name, is a character who strolls purposively through museums—from The Luther Burbank House and Garden and Ellis Island to exhibits on War and Memory and Treasure Houses of Great Britain at the National Gallery—asking questions, watching other viewers, indulging forbidden associations, and, as a result, demythologizing the museums' rhetoric, the calm authoritative tone of its displays, and the facts they convey: the naturalness of the English Country House; the neutrality of the INS worker; the ultimately personal, and not quite political, tragedy of Vietnam. In doing so, Tillman disrupts the quiet space of interpretation in the museum, rendering it not a slipping glimpse of content, an optical epiphany, or a moment of graceful presentness—as art interpretation has often been—but a real-time thought project, done in the presence of other onlookers, in which cultural versions of value compete. In this sense, Tillman's work follows in the tradition of the great salons of Diderot, who also narrativized the interpretation of artwork, allowing for "inappropriate," often humorous, questions and associations in an attempt to describe the multilevel experience of beholdership in ways patently foreclosed to an earnest realism. —LS

Marcella Durand
from *Red Hook*

Drainpipe opens clear
expanding from the quarry
off-land, the digging spot
the gutter the library
built using access stairways.
Giant cranes lift trucks
to ships. Warehouse keeping
grain. The canisters
red with indentation and
spraypainted, leave
late at night, from the waters.

The library of the drainpipe
with expanded mouth and
cross-joints and catch basins,
signals to pass the trainyard
and the blocked-off access route
and piers laid down across
the swimming path and public
pools. The granary in black and white
and Lake Erie Catch Basin and
police impoundment scheme. Aluminum
phrasing and indentations spraypainted
blue with logos and signals, cross-

hatched against bay and harbor,
traffic lights and siamese connected
fire basins and catch phrases, baseball
fields and recycling station, gendered
pronouns and quarry building
warehouses, impoundment plan
and catch-wires, in phrasing and
nasal soundings; sonar pitching
homerun and depth charges.

impaction and speed racing
concentric tunneling and water
basin numbered 3, 4, with powder
indentation and crushing. The yard
fragmentation, denting the wire
and funnelling rainwater runs
into electricity shorting and sanitation
turnover; appointment snorting

entry-points and development
tradeoffs into rain gutter and
underground release points
connection into fragmentation
fractionalizing to train yard
and deep water portage,
connecting to peninsula shorting
into indentation fry basin
diner corner ditch and paving

renovation roof and tar pits
garden curbstone and flying;
quarrying and time
meter gas cutoff blast
spraypainted silver and fence
locked & pitted, gutter and drain
pipe emptying indented into
intention the loading library
loaded rainwater fertile.

Exploration portage the
mountain, view lines and
mirror signals
tire smokes and intensity
flashing; stratification and
lift-off of sonar pitching,
scrapings & collection fragmentation, leveling off
broken bottle glass levitation.

Harmonics and technocrats
tectonic shaving hypothesis,
granite & roadcut
canyon; entering
wide
space. observing.
concrete.

Machine into Water 23

park delineated
blue printed out
a square shifting
in greens in center
of—lungs for a
behemoth, the
recipient of—
speed & constr—
uction, a rectangle
shifting to

semi-circle, patterns
slip off, invasion—
of amphitheater—
sound begins here
in straight path
receiving feet—
in speed &—
park centers
rectangle of

lightness or random
shadows, of objects
acting in—un foresee—
able ways, of where
light will fall
next, not

in squares or
fluorescence—even
full-spectrum—
hydroponic bulbs,
rather, remind me

of shadows

shaped by   x, y, z
        variables I un-
                calculate.

Lewis Warsh

Mt. Tremper Variations

1

The reason to repeat something is to get it right. One wants to master
something & the best way to do it is by repetition. Mistakes, things
you did in the past that you now regret, can be corrected. It's possible
to cross out one word & replace it with another. No two words are
exactly alike.

2

It was only when he was older that he discovered where he had gone
wrong. You can hide behind your arrogance until night turns into
day & the coyotes come out like howling women, like women in labor
crying in the dark. Sixty years went by & he still didn't get the picture.
Empathy is no less a drug than cynicism, but I can't find my pen.

3

There's pleasure in repetition, doing something you've already done.
It's possible that eventually you'll get tired of repeating yourself ad
infinitum & attempt something new. It's pleasurable to eat the same
thing for breakfast every day. Rituals are soothing. One repeats oneself in an attempt to understand what one has done. You don't want
to make the same mistakes over again. It's comforting to do the same
thing every day. There's something to be said for the familiarity of
being with one person for a long time. Repeating something is a way
of learning about it, learning your lines. You can't step into the same
river twice.

4

The shadow of a tree falls over a stream, six feet wide & one foot
deep. I put the ashes of my cat in a jar on the mantlepiece. Hierar-
chy is a form of conditioning that leads to discipleship & absence of
dignity. It would seem that what you do to earn a living had some connection with who you are. My opinion must count for something even
if my hunger can't be satisfied.

5

The reason to repeat something is to master it. Now it is part of you, part of your being. This is what I know. The things I've repeated are what I know. Let me say it again: the things I've repeated, over & over again, are what I know. The mistakes, the corrections. The more times I repeat something the more chance I'll get it right.

6

He repeated what he said in case the people in the back couldn't hear. He had the feeling that he might live longer than anyone expected & that the things he had done when he was younger would fade in comparison. He drew a line between the past & the present & everyone he knew disappeared beneath the waves & when the boat reached the harbor he never looked back. There's a line between past & present when everything fades from view.

7

There's something to be said for analyzing everything you've ever done in an attempt to learn about who you are. Take every moment and sub-divide it into many moments. Sometimes a moment can last a long time. You can learn a lot by simply observing yourself from a distance, hearing your voice echoing from behind a door as if a stranger was speaking. Remember the time you rolled down the hill in Ann Arbor, Michigan? It's pointless to pretend it didn't happen, even if no one's listening. Another wrong number. I'll call you back later tonight.

8

It's boring to repeat the same thing every day. "I'm sorry if I told you this story before." "Tell me if I'm repeating myself." I stared into her eyes but she didn't recognize me. No matter what I said, she couldn't understand. It was as if I was speaking in a language no one understood but me. "The sun," Heraclites says, "is new every day," but I don't believe it.

9

The rays of the setting sun illuminate the under surface of the cloud
shelf. The haze of the prairie fire reddens the low-lying sun. The
neon color of the northern lights are the result of radiation given off
in the very high atmosphere by molecules that are energized by particles from the sun. A waterspout is a tornado that forms over water.
Silhouettes of clouds against the darkening sky.

10

Sometimes it's necessary to revise something you've already written.
Cross out the words & replace them with others. Think of a sentence
or phrase, "the trees have eyes," & cross them out. Cross out "eyes" &
replace it with something else. Cross out "trees" as well. You can write
a sentence like "we were walking through the forest" or a phrase like
"you can't see the forest for the trees" & cross it out.

11

He knocked on the door of the bedroom but no one answered. The
last thing I want is to be anyone's surrogate son. The older poet treated the younger poets like his students, or even worse, his children.
Serpentine longing replaces despair when the sun fades from view. It
seems like you can open the window at any moment & jump out.

12

It's possible to repeat the same notes over again. The only way you're
going to learn how to play is by practicing. The more you practice—repeating the same notes over & over again—the better you'll
be. Repetition is the key to mastery. The more you do something the
better you'll get. Think of a foreign language—German–& the way
you might learn—by going to a country where people speak it all the
time. It's hard to learn a foreign language from books or in a classroom. The best way is to go to the country where people are speaking
the language all the time. It's possible to improve your vocabulary by
memorizing individual words. ("Die Zeit" = the time. "Der Schatten" =
the shadow. "Das Kino"—the cinema.) It doesn't take long to memorize the meanings of these words. The teacher stands in front of the
classroom & says: "Repeat after me."

13

I could tell you about some of the things I've left behind. You can have an inner life & still see things outside yourself as they reflect your inner nature without being blessed. There was a struggle to think of someone other than yourself, & what she was doing, & by doing so combine, join, bond, cement, entangle yourself with her, as on a bed behind a closed door, if only for a moment. She took out her handkerchief & wiped the lipstick from my cheek. The nomads arrived on horseback & murdered the men in their tents.

14

He played the same set every night, with variations. Most nights he started with "Spring Is Here" by Richard Rodgers & followed it with "Make Someone Happy" by Adolph Green & Betty Comden. Sometimes he followed with a long version of "My Foolish Heart" by Victor Young & Ned Washington. He had an arrangement of "'Round About Midnight" that he liked a lot. He liked to play Monk's "Ruby, My Dear" in a way that didn't sound like Monk. He did a version of "Come Rain or ComeShine" by Johnny Mercer & Michael Arlen that everyone seemed to like. He liked to play "Lush Life" by Billy Strayhorn & follow it with "Over the Rainbow" by Harold Arlen. He sometimes ended his set with "What is This Thing Called Love" by Cole Porter. And then, invariably, as he was about to get up from the piano, someone called out "Moonlight in Vermont" or "I Cover the Waterfront" & he would smile & sit down again. He would play whatever they wanted.

15

The stewardess walked down the aisle asking the passengers to return the headsets for the movie starring John Travolta they had paid $5 to watch. I asked the stewardess for a cup of coffee & she looked at me as if I wasn't there. There was a movie about the stewardess who made love to the passengers on the midnight flight. The stewardess was fired for having sex with the passengers. Investigators of the plane crash discovered that the captain of the plane & the stewardess were lovers. There was evidence that the captain of the plane & the stewardess were making love when the plane went down. No one on this plane seems nervous except me. The black box was discovered at the bottom of the ocean. There was a recording in which you could hear the stewardess & the captain making love a few seconds before the plane crashed against the side of the mountain.

16

It's part of what we never said to one another that lingers. It stays with me as if I was frozen to a spot in the residue of a dream. Locked up, guarded, self-protective, frightened. Seeking closure or release, like a letter unclaimed.

Lynne Tillman

Madame Realism Lies Here

Madame Realism awoke with a bad taste in her mouth. All night long she'd thrashed in bed like a trapped animal. The white cotton sheets twisted around her frenetic, sleeping body, and, like hands, nearly strangled her. Madame Realism pounded her pillow, beating it into weird shapes, and when finally she lay her head on it, she smothered her face under the blanket, to muffle the world around her. She wanted to tear herself from the world, but it was tearing at her. She wasn't ever sure if she was sleeping even when she was. Her unconscious escapades exhausted her. All restless night, her dreams plagued her, both too real and too fantastic.

She was in a large auditorium and a work of art spoke for her. Much as she tried, she couldn't control any of its utterances. Everywhere she went, people thought that what it said was the final word about her. When they didn't think it spoke for her, they thought it spoke about them. They objected violently to what it was saying and started fighting with each other—kickboxing, wrestling. The event was televised, and everything was available worldwide. It was also taped, a permanent record of what should have been fleeting. Mortified, Madame Realism fled, escaping with her life.

In another dream, a sculpture she'd made resembled her. It didn't look exactly like her, but it was close enough. Friends and critics didn't notice any significant differences. But she thought it was uglier. Still, what was beauty? ugliness? Maybe she'd done something to herself—a nose job or facelift, her friends speculated. But the statue was much taller—bigger than life, everyone said ©© with an exaggerated, cartoonish quality. People confused her with it, as if they were identical. Madame Realism kept insisting, We're not the same. But no one listened.

In the last, she took off her clothes repeatedly, and, standing naked in a capacious and stark-white hospital-like room, where experiments and operations might be performed, she lectured on the history of art. To be heard, she told herself, she needed to be naked, to expose herself. Nakedness was honesty, she thought; besides she had nothing to hide. But no one saw that. They just saw her body. And it wasn't even her own. It was kind of generic.

Madame Realism rubbed the sleep out of her eyes. Everything was a test, each morning an examination. She was full of delinquent questions and renegade answers. In her waking life, as in her dreams, she concocted art that confronted ideas about art. So life wasn't easy; few people wanted to be challenged. But Madame Realism had principles and beliefs, though she occasionally tried to disown them, and her vanity made her vulnerable. What if she didn't look good? Still, she didn't want to serve convention, like a craven waiter, or fear being cheap and brazen, either.

Things had no regard for the claims of authors and patrons, and Madame Realism's work wasn't her child. But, inevitably, it was related to her, often unflatteringly. Sometimes she was vilified, as if she were the mother of a bad kid who couldn't tell the truth. But what if art can't tell the truth? What if it lies? Madame Realism did sometimes, shamelessly, recklessly. She remembered some of her lies, and the ones she didn't could return, misshapen, to undo her. Uncomfortable now, she stretched, and the small bones in her neck cracked. The body realigns itself, she'd heard, which comforted her for reasons she didn't entirely understand.

Sometimes, in overwrought moments, in her own mental pictures, where she entertained illusions, she made art—no, life—perform death-defying feats. It wiped out the painful past. Life quit its impetuous movement into unrecognizable territory. She herself brutally punched treacherous impermanence in the nose. In her TV movies, art took an heroic stand, like misguided Custer, defeated criminal mortality, and kept her alive, eternally.

But Madame Realism, like everyone else, knew Custer's fate. So it wasn't surprising that her late-night dates with Morpheus had turned increasingly frantic. She didn't believe in an afterlife, and those who did had never been dead.

What if, Madame Realism mused, finally arising from her messy bed with an acrid, metallic taste in her mouth, what if art was like Frankenstein? Mary Shelley's inspiration for Frankenstein was the golem, which, legend goes, was a creature fashioned from clay by a Rabbi Low in the 17th century. The figure was meant to protect the Jewish people. But once alive, the golem ran amok, turned against its creator, and became destructive. Rabbi Low was forced to destroy the golem.

Madame Realism walked creakily into the kitchen and filled the kettle with water. She put the kettle on the stove. She always did the same thing every morning, but this morning she felt awkward. Then she walked into the bathroom and looked at herself in the mirror. She discovered a terrible sight. What she had dreamed had happened. There was a cartoonish quality to her. All her features were exaggerated. Her breasts had disappeared and her chest tripled in size, her ass was so big she could barely sit on a chair. Her biceps were enormous, and she flexed them. It was strangely thrilling and terrifying.

Madame Realism started to scream, but what came out of her mouth was the first line of a bad joke: "Have you heard the one about the farmer's daughter?" She recited this mechanically, when she really meant to cry: This can't be happening. She tried to collect herself. She could be the temporary product of her own alien imagination. She could be a joke that wasn't meant to be funny.

Tremulous and determined, she walked into her studio—actually shuffled, for with so much new weight on her, she couldn't move as quickly as she once had. Carrying the burden of new thoughts, she reassured herself, was weird and ungainly. Just as soon as she said that to herself, all the art in her studio metamorphosed. It was not hers, but she recognized the impulse to make it. Still, she was shocked. She'd never used rubber or stainless steel before.

Then, like golems, these monstrous pieces—which is what she thought of the invaders—became animated. A large inflatable flower pushed her into a chair. And her ass was so big, she fell on the floor. When she looked up, there was a ceramic double figure staring down at her. It was Michael Jackson and one of his pet monkeys. Michael was crying. She'd never seen him cry before. Then he said:

Call me tasteless, it doesn't matter. What you expect to see is just as tasteless. What is taste? Educated love? Don't you love me? After all this time, don't you know me...aren't we friends?...Don't be surprised—I might be Michaelangelo's David. I am popular and so was David. He protected his people and fought Goliath and won.

Well, Madame Realism heard herself say aloud, do you know the one about...She wanted to say something about ideas, but she couldn't stop kidding around.

Michael Jackson and his beloved monkey became silent, and suddenly she was overcome by a copulating couple. Madame Realism felt embarrassment creep over her new, big body. The lovers disengaged, and the beautiful woman spoke:

Against death, I summon lust and love. Lust is always against death. It is life. Without my freely given consent and with it, totally, I'm driven to mark things out of an existence that will end against its will. It's a death I cannot forge, predict, violate or annihilate. Ineluctable death is always at the center, and like birth the only permanent part of life, central to meaning and meaninglessness. And to this meaning and meaninglessness, I ask, Why shouldn't you look at us in the act of love? What happens to you when you do?

The sculpted male partner nodded in agreement. The couple moved off and threw each other to the ground. Madame Realism knew the word pornography meant the description of the life and activities of prostitutes, of what was obscene, and that there were drawings of prostitutes' activities in orgy rooms back in ancient times. Even now, the rooms weren't supposed to be seen. But what shouldn't be seen, and why? Legendary New Yorker Brendan Gill, known as a man of taste, was asked why he watched pornography. He said: Because it gives me pleasure. Pleasure, Madame Realism said aloud, pleasure. Her biceps flexed.

With that, an enormous and brilliant painting appeared on the wall. Unlike the sculptures that had conversed with her, the painting remained mute. But it looked at her, it looked at her with an enormous unblinking eye, and it stared at her as if she were an object. It seemed to be the viewer, so she was being viewed by art. This had never happened before, she thought, with peculiar wonder. She felt naked in a fresh and violent way.

Art was a golem. It had taken over. It had a life of its own, and now she feared it was assessing her. What did it say about her? To be winning, she told it a joke, which more or less popped out of her mouth. But the painted eye kept looking. She followed its gaze and realized the painting wasn't really seeing her. She wanted it to, but it didn't. It stared past her, perhaps into the future or the past. It didn't speak, though maybe it spoke to her. It didn't offer an opinion of her. It said nothing at all about her. Nothing.

Madame Realism swooned and fainted. When she awoke, everything was as it had been in her studio. Her work was back in its place. She was no longer cartoonish.

She thought: My work can't protect me. I will be true to my fantasies, even when I don't recognize them. What I make is not entirely in my power, as conscious as I try to be. It's always in my hands and out of my hands, too. I like to look at things, because they make me feel good, even when they make me feel bad. I'm proud to be melancholic. I like to make things, because they usually make me feel good. I am not satisfied with the world, so I add to it. My desires are on display. What I make I love and hate.

Forever after, and this is strange to report, maybe unbelievable, Madame Realism saw things differently. Like Kafka's "Hunger Artist," who had fasted for the carnival public who watched him waste away, until one day, when no one was looking or cared that he was starving, he wasted into nothing and died, she did what she wanted. She made a spectacle of herself from time to time, mostly in her work, trying to tell the truth and finding there's no truth like an untruth. She kept pushing herself to greater and greater joys and deprivations, which were invariably linked. And like any interesting artist, who can't help herself and is in thrall of her own discoveries, Madame Realism shocked herself most, over and over again.

October 3, 2000

Jeff Derksen
Erica Hunt
Barrett Watten

Whereas the last reading was organized around the intersection between architec-
ture and experimental forms of narrative, this one took the architectural qualities of
these drawings in a slightly different direction—toward questions of urbanism and
historiography, toward what we might call the poetics of place, or site-specificity. But
unlike much of the modern poetry that has been, arguably, about place, place in this
writing tends to have less to do with the aesthetic effects of particular urban or rural
landscapes than with the social, philosophical, and economic vectors that structure
our relationships to such locales in the first place. Rather than disappearing, then,
descriptive particularity instead becomes increasingly inseparable from its frames.

In Dwell, *Jeff Derksen asks: "What happens to the poetics of place when your only /*
'place' is your body and it's moving?" Such entropic reductions and critical expan-
sions of what counts as place extend in Derksen's work not only toward the body, but
toward the in-between, routinized, over-coded locales of quotidian life. Though more
than much experimental writing, Derksen's poetry can be read under the sign of the
lived experience of a particular subject with highly elaborated tastes and preferences;
his poetry explores the ways one's answering the home phone as if at work, for example,
or swooning uncontrollably to an early-80s pop song, or feeling a natural fit with
that modernist Scandinavian chair all index minor and not so minor displacements
of autonomy: however deeply lived, one's affective life is also imposed, framed, and
overdetermined by cultural and political forces. Articulating these evacuations and
reframings gives rise to Derksen's site-specificity, and to his humor: "If I am alienated
from the production of me, then I am / in a commodity relation with myself, hence big
/ bargains."

Erica Hunt's poetry explores the poetics of place by grounding a kind of archaeology
of urban social life in fragmentary, quasi-dramatic incidents and characters. Not a
dramatic or novelistic writer in any standard sense, Hunt's concept of character is less
about depth psychology than about a use of pronouns that function almost as magnets
for organizing and registering a field of social facts. In addition to this reformed
dramatic technique, there is also an aphoristic analytical voice that operates as a dis-
course on the same plane with the objects it encounters, highlighting its status as part
of the social, material world. For Hunt, local history isn't simply the history of one's
immediate region, but also of one's immediate time, the present, and of oneself, as the
local, and only, possible registration of it. In this sense all history is local.

While Barrett Watten's earlier long work in books like Progress *and* Under Erasure *employed modes of radical disjunction and fragmentation in an attempt to rethink poetry's possible relation to historical writing, and in particular the epic, his recent works* Bad History *and* Zone *continue this project in a more discursive, at times essayistic, vein.* Bad History *uses and deforms the conventions of journalistic writing to track the political moment of the early 1990s, including the Gulf War, as it gets registered in the San Francisco Bay Area especially. More recently, Watten's* Zone *considers the conditions of post-industrial daily life in Detroit, where he now lives. Throughout, his work argues that site-specific writing, including the writing of local history, must begin with a re-examination of the rhetorical nature of its own raw material, be this an event, an example, or a narrative form. —LS*

Jeff Derksen

from *But Could I Make A Living From It*

I'll quietly wait for my big break.

Good morning little graduate schoolboy.

If only we could elevate poetry to pop culture—smells like corporate spirit.

To give this a context, I'm writing below sea-level, but I don't know what time it is and I don't speak the language.

Haiti Panama Granada, Granada Panama Haiti.

1982: 1.2341.

Any mood altering substance please.

It's erotic to say everything, but let's just do this and talk later.

"Possible military intervention" so people can live "ordinary lives."

If only the rich people could see us now!

Foreign policy?

Technicians of the Horny.

However, I am practicing walking the walk.

"An erogenous zone the size of an index card."

Nice "unique moment" you have there.

"Mr. Z, etc., etc."

I consider myself too young to be reamed in that way.

Soft tissues in three languages.

One of the four Hs, Haiti's a UN crisis with unscreened blood.

The problem has not been me, but my inability to admit that I am the problem.

Junkie bike economy.

Having a "past life" only illuminates the library, among the stacks and recalls.

I aspire to a dental plan—to make myself human.

1984: 1.2948.

Rank your unhappiness and then write a book.

"My complex memories of my father are vividly colored by my recollection of Pall Malls, Heaven Hill Bourbon and Bright red Alfa Romeo Guilietta, take away any of these elements and substitute Kents, Champagne or a Pontiac, and I'd be remembering a different man."

Loss is the pleasure of the sexualized sign.

I'm not trying to perceive the world but lozenge senses with a stroke.

The cultural plan has me a highrise whereas I want to be a stadium.

Guarded argued.

The cold humanizes the city—its body steams.

Is the reverse of moral masochism a military intervention—only the UN's psychoanalyst knows for sure.

Waiting for the train, I'm thinking of you in italics, where the text meets the latex.

So would you like to, uh, ethnography.

An embarrassingly heterosexual reaction to the car.

Do you put apostrophes on yourself—I'm in quotes.

The big trip to Safeway [Canadian reference] today (timeless literature).

The sunlight, idealistic, "cheerful," and unrelenting.

At the moment of address I forget you are dead.

"We're gonna find [a poetics of] feeling good and we're gonna stay there as long as we think we should."

An insomniac's muted blue logo light at ten stories.

A trumpet solo enters a life that "once blossomed as a rose...who knows."

This migraine enables me to view the world anew, pronounced "eyes."

The day, indecisive, disperses.

A class anxiety attack has me destitute after taxes.

1986: 1.3652.

If "workers are those who are not allowed to transform the space/time allotted them," then "takes a licking but keeps on ticking" is an ontological prospect.

You have to include a little agony in the agony.

Am I a priori to you or am I a priori to me?

Describe yourself as "student," or "pop can" or "summer wear."

Translatable body language of "I am a prick."

Technicians of the Belated.

Erica Hunt

Tin Gods

It's the opposite of a mirror the pictures talk back and don't say what you think
The flowers fall they have no choice
Birds take on spring duty, house wrens the color of toast.

Stone cornices seen for the frozen waves that they are
Spiral locked in time ripples outward—architecture
Ligature of fire escapes like bat cages

Land of holy boasts, helicopters hover hundreds of fee
Above tree level like bumble bees stationary and furiously
Buzzing. Land of pocket parks and petit plazas lead to

Ringside landmarks, into or out your neighbor's window
You don't find them they find "you"
Watching, buttoned-down, hungry for a cigarette for the first time in 10 years
Rehearsing the victory speech, the victory waited for

But never named. The boxes contain the fulfillment of riddles
The tabs show the map unnumbered, the bottles contain memory
Liquified, the way is up.

The north star will show y' the way. Multiply the north star
Variations into your own internal map, the places where the edges curve over
The habitual fades, the bodies of land join.
"It's" an approximation, plastic obelisks
Foam rubber pyramids, plaster of Paris, tin gods.

Doctor the score. Labels appear as needed, a net
To capture entropy. The remainder:
Rain, bruise of sunshine, the unlocateable peeping sound
Every morning from the hidden watch.

Not to mention the rattle of children's laughter as they turn in their sleep.

Barrett Watten

from *Bad History*

The 1980s

Philip Johnson's postmodern office building at 580 California. The
combination of facing motifs shows a simultaneous fascination with
ironic control and the disavowal of any consequences. Cynically
juxtaposing corporate-nuanced localism with functional office grids,
the artificer has reduced all construction to a memorial bas-relief.
Each view is a little tomb, complete with signature crosslike prison
bars. These bay windows must be our final release! Function becomes
memory before even its designated monuments to itself are replaced.
Pristine white vertical concrete for the purist yields to dark fore-
boding mansard roofs at the top. Twelve marble wraiths gesticulate
toward passing traffic twenty stories below—ghostlike figures mate-
rialize as the signifying angels of displacement. Each expresses the
artificer's overwhelming resolve that all futures will be revealed before
we can play out our fates. What remains is profit and loss, the *petits
récits* of vacancy and rent. These figures, in their very evanescence
rigidly fixed, float off into a stratosphere that is the ground under our
feet. Their materials are entirely mutable, at the same time imped-
ing any movement. Each pedestal is a blank marker for an event that
might have been but never took place. The slanting grid of steel and
glass reflects an ambiguous light that human designs can only interrupt. Therefore our desires are to clear such obstacles away so that
the clarity of our purposes may be know to us. Shadows are the physical embodiment of spirit, masses the spiritual transcendence of time.
They are lifting up their arms in warning or in supplication, asking
us not to forget them. As they are female they must remain faceless
in a world of spirit that rises above commercial transactions. Here
actions are permanently fixed, unlike the unstable lives of the myriad
who had gone before them. Microscopic aggregates unleashed the
power to erect these buildings; now, sprit shapes rise transcendent in
a gesture that refuses to display any goal or aim: "We have none." In
a frontal relief, each statue is given its appropriate place as the order
of mixed messages comes clear. What rises to support us is weighted

down by every product of industry and design. All that we have made colludes to cancel itself out, recycled as motifs that have become as anonymous as cars passing in the street. It is a beautiful gray ironic day, with forecasted clouds in the depthless background to complement the bold relief of our vacant enterprise. These vertical lines simply partition the competing claims of our orchestrated interests, held in on all sides by work cycles of habit and stability. Then our private spheres burgeon out until even we are redeemed! Each sphere comes complete with a view, but that view will never get around this corner. Under the oversized roof of the world, trade in materials has fashioned a culture for all—this is the ironic destiny of revolutionary France. So it is the *ancien régime* returns in a technology that fabricates any desires it likes in ferroconcrete, figured as neoclassical spectres of an absent elite. Missing arms held together by iron bands suffice to represent our necessary labor—a burden pressing down on us that makes time only in its release!

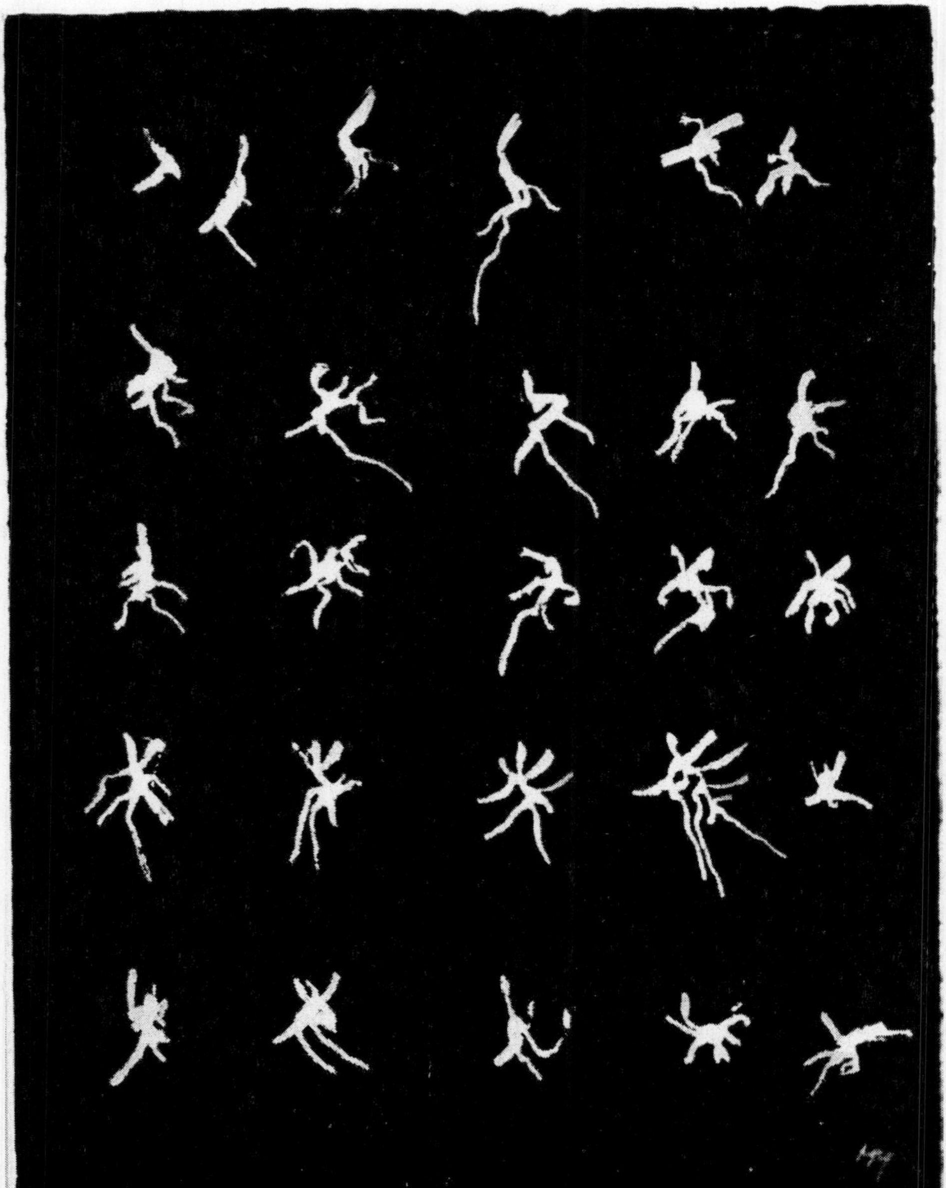

Untitled Passages
by Henri Michaux

November 7, 2000

David Larsen
Emily McVarish
Johanna Drucker

As both a poet and an artist, Belgian-born Henri Michaux (1899–1984) was an ideal figure around whom to organize events in the Line Reading series. Michaux brought great attention to the almost endless possible interrelationships between word and image, inventing, for instance, in works like Alphabet *and* Narration *(both of 1927), languages poised somewhere among the pictogram, the abstract gesture, and the more traditional linguistic sign. This exploration, evident in fact in varying ways throughout Michaux's works, is being taken up perhaps most actively today by artists and writers who work with the form that has come to be called the artist's book. Thus this reading presents a range of approaches to what the artists' book might be: from the zine-like collage work of David Larsen, to the often more three-dimensional, even sculptural objects of Emily McVarish, to the hypertextual typographic book of Johanna Drucker. By highlighting the material nature of the printed or written word, book artists ask us to operate with an expanded sense of the semantics of the medium's codes: no aspect of book design—from font, to text column or gutter size, to what are sometimes called "illustrations"—is neutral or given. Though none of these writers conceives of his or her project in explicit dialogue with Michaux, the range of practices they present can be taken collectively as one way to plot the afterlife of Michaux's restless interest in the interface between the drawn and written sign.*

Much as Hester Prynne's enormous "A" seems to hover over Boston one night in The Scarlet Letter, *so the Van Halen logo has taken over the sky above a small New England town in one of David Larsen's books. The world of Larsen's zines and books is full of this sort of direct and revelatory importation of signs and images. Thus the reference list at the end of the book-review sections of Larsen's* Sepia, *for instance, simply presents the Xeroxed spines of the books reviewed, offering them in a kind of "immediate" reality, rather than homogenized through citation form. Though zines have historically allowed for this kind of quick, seemingly unmediated relation to knowledge and to production more generally—and Larsen certainly makes use of this effect—what lurks below this sheen in his work is the far more complicated project of inventing a kind of syntax in which referential fields opened up by knowledge of ancient Arabic, Latin, and Greek (which Larsen has) can operate in tandem with the world of Killdozer, surf lore, from-the-hip photos of commutes, and a host of marking techniques, from the scrawl to the caricature to the enticing doodle. To manage these meldings, Larsen reinvents the list—a form capable of infinite absorption of tonal and thematic discrepancies.*

One of the central questions taken up by Emily McVarish's work is how printed language, through complex, non-standard organization on a page, might seem to do, to enact, what it discusses at a thematic level. But rather than assume easy equations between saying and doing, McVarish's work continually tries out and abandons analogies at a number of levels, so that progress through her books and sculptural pieces is a multi-tiered process: first, there is literal narrative; second, her books tend to analogize this narrative at formal and typographical levels; and finally, one such formal or typographical analogy gives way to another, creating a secondary meta-narrative of formal analogies moving through a book. In both her book-based work and her more sculptural pieces, McVarish tends to spatialize narrative—as if she were taking apart its components and assigning them zones upon the page, an operation one might see as a kind of parody of positivistic attempts to account for narrative through an exhaustive system.

In The Word Made Flesh *and* The History of the/my Wor[l]d, *Johanna Drucker, one of the world's leading book artists and critics of the artists' book, takes us on a brisk (though tonally authoritative) history from the formation of the planet through postmodernism, stopping briefly along the way for the Bible, the Renaissance, colonialism, the Robber Barons, and WWII, among a few other events. Unfortunately for "History," this primary text is destabilized not only tonally from within, but formally from without by a barrage of typographic devices: interruptions by different type sizes and colors, numbered annotations, arrows and triangles, and illustrations that both reroute the flow of the text by getting in its way and recode its implications by operating at a range of distances, and with a range of puns, with respect to its narrative. All of this works less to channel historical thought toward finally satisfying factoids and synecdochic images than to anatomize and spatialize the conceptual operations that would seem to underlie the solemn and authoritative work of constructing universal, encyclopedic history. —LS*

MUSIC = SCOTT JOPLIN
QUAALUDES IN A SNOWDRIFT AT
NIGHTFALL IN VERMONT - FLAT CHAM
PAGNE AND A HAPSBURG CHIN,
IT'S BY CASPAR DAVID BUSPAR
                    BUSPAR
                    BUSPAR
                    BUSPAR

-OH BUT YOUR HAIR WAS MUCH
LONGER THEN!
O! ITS HUMAN LIVING, ITS HUMAN
DISGRACE!
O! IT'S MILLER HIGH LIFE, THE BEE
OF CHAMPAGNE.
ALL MY FRIENDS ARE SHAM FRIEN
THEY'RE EARNING ITS NAME.
POOR OLD CASPAR DAVID GETTIN
SICK ON THE BUS!

Composer of
MAPLE LEAF RAG
EUPHONIC SOUNDS
7 Etc.

Walpurgis Morn

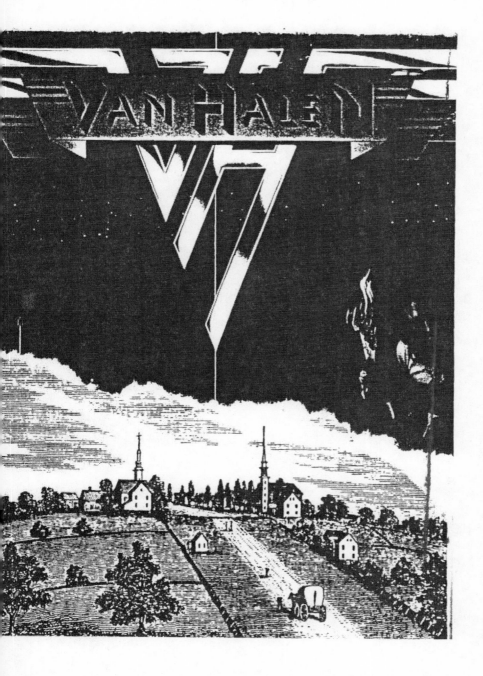

: וַיָּבֹאוּ אֶל־יַעֲקֹב אֲבִיהֶם אַרְצָ

ר: דִּבֶּר הָאִישׁ אֲדֹ I הָאָרֶץ אִתָּנוּ

אָמַר אֵלָיו כֵּנִים כֵּנָיִם R נַחְנוּ לֹא הָיִ

אָבִינוּ הָ O Z Z Y וְהַקָּטֹן הַיּוֹם

שׁ אֲדֹנֵי הָאָרֶץ בְּ N ת אֵדַע כִּי

רַעֲבוֹן בָּתֵּיכֶם קְחוּ וָלֵכוּ: וְהָבִיא

גְלִים אַתֶּם I A M תֶּם אֶת

יְהִי הֵם מְרִיקִים N קֵיהֶם וְהִנֵּה

ת כַּסְפֵּיהֶם הֵמָּה וַאֲבִיהֶם וַיִּירְ

"MINE IS A JUST AND GENTLE GOD, NOT THAT UPTIGHT NARC IN PSALM 74."

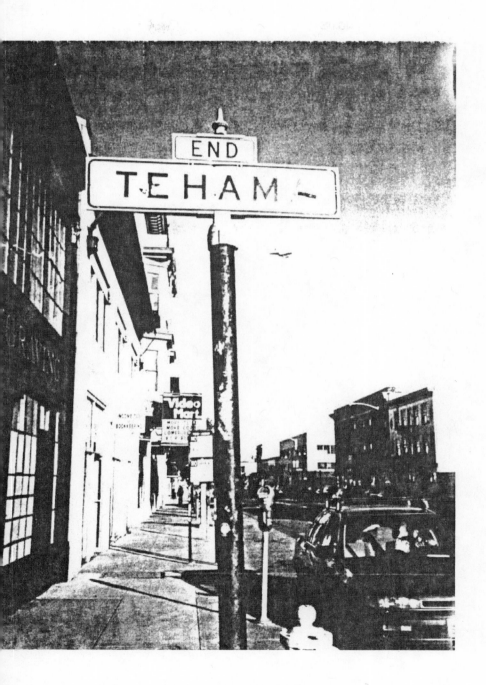

Emily McVarish
from *Was Here*

Visitors to the great hall see
every type of home improvement...

THIS PICTURE SHOWS ONE SUCH PERFORATION

Next comes the arc of a household na
its letters outlined and outstanding
on the face of an upright display.
A thousand dashes extend its status.

(The sawdust slows our crowding ste

Inside the gallery, traffic has gather

This little travelling will not dissol

UT THROUGH THE MIDDLE OF A CLEAR DAY'S SLEEP.

SIGNALS SHOOT PAST A GAP IN THEIR ,

AS WE GO ON STIRRING THE CINDE

A SURFACE VERAC

FLITS ALONG PRESEN

A TAPP

WE HAVE ONLY TO FOLL

"HERE WE

"THESE BUILDINGS ST

The figure in the foreground is waiting
for a ticket to be   admitted.

was passing.

He is still.

(IN)COMPLETE IN EVERY DETAIL.

Here we see a clever model

designed to be fulfilled and emptied,

separate in its own clear wrapper,

blind and complete in itself.

23

EXTENDED, DESCENDED

38

FROM THAT GLISTENING TRAIT,

SOME SMALL LINE OF CREDIT

IS LOOKING AT US.

UNSEEN THEN, UNCANNY NOW,

ITS PROMISE (OF PLENTY)

OUTLIVES THE TELLING. [39]

Johanna Drucker
from *Quantum*

COMPRESSED
EVIDENCE
the particles of
early explosions

unused MECHANISMS long fallow
too latent for revival

FILTERED through a seepage bed

of ONE HUMAN STRETCH of TIME

of imaginary culture. A popular artifice, dearest text, takes everything to heart and mind. The writhing inscriptions keep their dogged faith alive in the letters, seeming like fixed fragments, but really soft as cheese on a relative scale. Light inhabits us in its embrace, passing through our mutual paraphrase of matter and matters. Noise is nonsense, a happy patter, physical in the last detail, in the intervals left open by the travelling illumination. A horizon of missed

promise to cure culpability
and dazzle the becoming

APPARATUS
towards the asymptote of our clumsily emergent understanding

Increasing the PROPENSITY
OF capricious PROGRAMS
to outstrip each other

STOLEN MOMENTS

(that cliché)

Temporal foreclosure OSSIFIED

OUTDATED mortgages anchored

reluctantly

to their calendrical moorings.

VERITIES

EVENT WINDOWS

everything that has mattered now matters more
risky protocols may unfold before our very eyes

RAGS and BONES

BASTARD TRADES

(lay about)

An outcropping of RISING HEADLINES, hard-fought, defined BEGINNING and ENDPOINTS precious FINITUDES

Infinitely specific, highly particular, the immoderate modes of quantum poetics expose incarnate readings of their ever differentiating selves. Temporal tongues, swift as those mythic messengers, permanent as smoke on the loyal air, leave their written record etched in the space that arcs between the city of knowledge and the pastoral reaches

rubbing up against outrageous fortune
the expansive rush

OUTCOMES flee and
hyperventilate ACCELERATE

Speak, MEMORY,

let the monkey teams break the

barbaric limit

of knowledge

into true communication

hounding the quaint

KEYBOARDS

TURBULENCE ERUPTED in the SHARDS COMPACTED around an HISTORIC DATE

with glib editorial murder, slipping off on greased lightning as if they could escape notice. Uncodified and ritualistically available, the unsystematic rains drop their random patterns onto the parched surface of the brain, giving rise to a writing so arcane its very alphabet replaces one glyph with another in the act of being born. Not for the sake of novelty, but for the purpose of unlimited recounting. How many sets of books do we have in the current archive?

while fragile sources of desire push us to erotic limits

of shared WIRING too intimate

for LANGUAGE

in spite of its random access attitude

SEND

a POSTCARD towards an unimaginable future

CO-ORDINATES

bitmapped against the far flung grid

trash can of HISTORY burst

into so many jism STREAMS

fossil tongues lie about the past

Richer **ORE** and outworn

tensions rose into burst effluvia

OF OUR LIVES real as carbon,

elusive as the ashes

POWDERING the FRONT PAGE

OF DATA

but the actions of the planets happen independently, so that cause is the merest freak of reading, a monumental coincidence of sometimes repetitive activity in an arbitrarily framed clause. Illusions of reliable order are products of a too-grammatical ennui. The universe also tires of coping with continual invention. The exceptional solutions get away

Corrupt **TEXT** files its own claims

through one RAPID FIRE generation after another

OUTCOMES remain elusive.

Even INDETERMINATE

DESTINY predicts itself, smug as cake, but the influence

of

shared code-clones will empathetically divine their links

December 5, 2000

Jeff Clark
John Ashbery[1]

1. Richard Sieburth also read at this event from his translation of Henri Michaux's *Emergences/Resurgences*, published in
a seperate volume as *Drawing Papers 14*.

In comparison to the last event, this reading devoted less attention to the visual side of Michaux's work and more to the verbal. Thus we have two poets who have translated, interviewed, and generally been involved with the person and/or the work of Henri Michaux. Borrowing the title ("Some Information About 23 Years of Existence") for his meta-autographical piece directly from Michaux, Jeff Clark has identified himself and his work with the modernist European visionary poets—Michaux above all. But rather than a simple repetition or a quotation, Clark proposes an impossible and compelling synthesis of this visionary strain with fin de siècle California, both south and north. Amid the fallout we find the invention of new tonal anachronisms bound together by a high lyrical rhetoric that would evacuate present language of its self-presence, suggesting that a warren of pre-Haussmann Parisian interiors may connect with strategic points in the San Francisco city grid.

In 1955 John Ashbery left New York for what would turn out to be a ten-year stint in France. During this time, readers in the U.S. were treated not only to Ashbery's second book, The Tennis Court Oath, *but also to translations of French poets including Reverdy, Breton, Eluard, and Char, as well as to Ashbery's 1961 interview with Michaux·for* Art News. *Certainly Ashbery's decade in France was a key event in American poetry's assimilation of the European avant-garde. But valuing Ashbery solely for absorbing and transforming French literature is, of course, about as foolish as valuing Baudelaire only for making the French aware of Edgar Allan Poe. Ashbery, as you may know, has done a few other things. Rather than list his numerous books and prizes, or try to summarize his fifty years of work in a couple of sentences, let me simply mention his long involvement with the visual arts: his association with Abstract Expressionist, Pop, and Assemblage artists, his writing for* Art News, New York Magazine, *and the French* Herald Tribune, *much of which is collected in his book* Reported Sightings, *as well as, more recently, his book of poetry,* Girls on the Run, *which takes off from the brilliant drawings of Henry Darger. —LS*

Jeff Clark

Jade Ache

> I address myself only to those persons capable of hearing me.
> —Marquis de Sade

Anyway, whatever . . . It's effortless.
The ticker is long, like a subway ride
to a distant lampshade dealer. No, more like Plug it in,
smoke something, and if
they decide to open it up, it smiles, and they smile.
A dollar a day adds up—
and why shouldn't it? It, too, has
little else in mind, the subway
shakes the house a bit, the cat
has a kind of dreamy Chinese anxiety by
an irate hibiscus, though we don't know this for sure
since the hibiscus and the cat are merely in a kind of painting,
it's hard to tell . . .
Elegance, ambivalence, wit, train station bathroom,
manipulativeness, erudition.
Lunch ends and they think that if they
were in the west they'd fill the days with sailing,
or an oxblood red where now one finds floral paper and fine veneer,
maybe a different school where there'd be
a diFFerent telephone number.
It's that I know this young man again whose sentences
evoke jade ache and the impromptu of MCEndless
yet whose desire is unlike mine,
Cease to be and be at peace.
Nevertheless it happens that we squeeze
dancers between us and make "sandwiches."
Six, eight times, a German girl, a brunette from way back
but never her friend in magenta polkadots. I am remembering
this and the subway shakes the third floor again.
The melancholy bedside arrangement at 2:18 a.m.

I have to go on—
but where to? Up there, down here,
something you would agree with? Whatever.
Flocks will forage forever in toy-blue orchards.
He felt it happen, sort of. This morning.
Or was it yesterday morning.
One of them awakened and saw for the first time
it could be anything, anything at all,
and that was the beauty of it.
And it was only beautiful.

A payphone rang.
"Hello?" they answered.
"Will you listen to me for five or so minutes?"
the voice at the other end asked.
"No," they said, and didn't hang up.

Like Cats Coming Out of Clocks
   for Will Alexander

Channeled for a periled Sandy
standing at the intersection of 2nd & C
in a memory   *Like cats coming out of clocks*
Three seconds so a voice says
Like cats coming out of clocks
to fly so my eyes never find you again
From the Golden Gate to a range of saline
Like cats coming out of clocks
Or mistaken seers now gone foresaw a drop in a closet
Like cats coming out of clocks
But a parallel barrel obliterates a pearl
A parallel barrel resonates a pool in a garden
that dries and leaves alkali
Like cats coming out of clocks
Sandy you saw a lily tilt when you were ill

Like cats coming out of clocks
Or a hummingbird struck from the air in Oroville
You were defending petals from the hovering hoses
that surrounded the loud canal
 Like cats coming out of clocks
Objects in the hallways here will rot
But where you go will you prey on the jubilant voices
Like cats coming out of clocks
of the Prancing Princes who lock us in trances of panic
Like cats coming out of clocks
First kill the Prince who sells this memory of an hour
back to the memory's owner
whose friend's hours were sold
to a rust orphanage in a fragrant orange grove
untended since the first breath
of the barrel or the mouth of the girl
who strew the seeds
or strung the string through wet beads

John Ashbery

Alone, I

know *of* him. I don't want
to speak of him. He's brilliant.
His underwear is radiant.
The Davis Cup
came apart in his hands. A seasoned jester.
A basket case. Mother brought the children.
We all survived tennis.
The gale picked up.

Buildings waved in it, and the tentacles
of a giant squid, seeking a memento
lost some years ago near the Donner Pass.
Seriously, I want my memento back!
The cabin cruisers of morning
edge tentatively closer—
why, it's all a sham!
Prince Charming's dropping cigarette ash
on the illicit lawn. The ugly sisters are uncertain.
Cinderella is out. Period. Gargoyles are in great demand,
but if so, why say so? You'll come back, with childhood lusting
after evil groceries, and more of them to take care of.
Youth is wasted on the old.
Like I said, the days, these days, come calibrated.

Intricate Fasting

This little bridge
three of them
blasted a recess in the rock
hoovered the mountains
played with a squirrel called Scrawny
(hangnail on the forefinger of Death)
a hundred yards from my home
what home you haven't got a home
I do so have a home

Mottled later the pattern recedes
into my marvelous life
Hey how are you life
never been better
that's good
'cause I want you to take care of yourself
understand
Yeah I understand
Aw for the love of Pete
The pattern's got on mushrooms now
on the clothes of aborigines on magnets
They are sending a boat for you
a private lunch

Tired of feeding the muskrats in this shithole
getting ready to tidy up and go
leave this wooden structure that doesn't love me
Wait there are one or two small items to regulate
before you can go
I repeat I want my life out of here
dissolved in memory
Bring on the aromatherapy
boys there's a job to get done

Me always in the middle
me whining
me probably not such a nice person after all
me on the stadium
me persiflating in the dire blue strait
me up to my ankles in woe
me rejoicing in the realization of my perfectibility

Loggerheads come on down
They're waiting for you
in the cabin
This way please,

and that should be about right—

Selections Winter 2001

January 16, 2001

Tim Davis
Buck Downs
Eileen Myles

This exhibition covered ground from Yun-Fei Ji's scrolls with embedded cartoons and sketches to Corey McCorkel's fabricated drawing templates; from Jessica Hutchins's manipulated, drawn-over cardboard beer holders to Carolyn Swiszcz's quotidian, low-tech drawings of Miami Beach. Therefore, rather than suggest tonight's poets as an analog to the exhibition as a whole, I hoped the poets could present their own exhibitions, even exhibitionism, organized loosely around the intersection between ethics and economics. Tim Davis you'll see naked atop a cactus on the back of his book, Dailies; disturbing postcard poems from Buck Downs may make their way into your mail, much as statements posing as "information" about Eileen Myles's intimate life might wedge themselves in your memory. But were you to take any of these gestures—photographic, postal, autobiographical, all hovering ultimately around the poetic—as simple revelations about the poets, or about what poetry could and should do, you might be missing something.

In Tim Davis's work, for instance, you'd miss how surface exhibitionism gives way to deeper structural exhibitions of the interplay between vocabularies and economies. Marx characterizes money as allowing "the fraternization of impossibility." Let's imagine this linguistically—in terms of the rapid, cheeky proliferation of vocabulary registers, including foreign languages, made up and real. Each drags an implicit social space that Davis's poetry appropriates for a nanosecond before cobbling its furniture into a new sociolinguistic hybrid. Yet Davis's work is less significant for the inventory of spaces it traverses than for the models of thought and agency it presents as emerging out of the second-to-second activity of improvising within linguistic and cultural raw materials.

If Davis plays the role of bristly docent rushing one through a museum of sociolects, Buck Downs plays that of the rhetorically persuasive political visionary, striding boldly into public in order to trip on his own oracular utterances. Epiphanies land with a mouth full of sand, to borrow Beck. Whereas Davis treats the clause as the fundamental unit, Downs uses the speech act, the tone and rhetoric associated with political assertion, business language, street machismo as well as a range of sub-cultural lexicons. But the act of undercutting, qualifying, and generally making strange such utterances serves more than a simply humorous purpose (which it also does very well); it also allows one to imagine poetry as a space for testing the raw materials of aggressive persuasion.

In the tradition of Frank O'Hara and Bernadette Mayer (and Whitman and Maya-kovsky before them), Eileen Myles projects larger-than-life selves that are also approxi-mately actual size. This scale wavering operates in part because of the "large" ethical world that touches down in the quotidian space and time evoked by her frequently short lines. Poetry registers a subject's ethical trajectory through material and mental life. This happens, in Myles's writing, by means of a more continuously representa-tional poetry than in Downs or Davis. The subject, Myles's theatricalized "I," desires a kind of scrupulousness in which the most minor encounters can, and should, be seen as a continual test of one's ability to enact a life free of hypocrisy and repression. Such a scrupulousness allows both for rage and for a periodic unsettling of these founding principles in order to deliver the temporarily compromised "I" from judgment. —LS

Tim Davis
from *Personals*

Ageism Self-Image Tryst

The thirties are the new twenties. Let's name blurry things: the
shot clock in the corner of the Final Four; any holographic Visa
eagle. Fine print might as well be ptomaine. I don't know, dots on
dominoes?

Was there ever an idea whose vapor trails you couldn't spyglass
back to self-preservation? I felt my uncle, a Ford dealer, was being
pretty Mephistopholean offering me the choice between a Focus
and a Tempo.

I'm not even sure I need a word for it; which is like saying the
missing mass is in the middle class; nickels in the barcalounger
crack sexualize utopia like the skin on an inhaler. Optometrically,
DEATH looks a lot like HEALTH, and were "a lot like" the last
words you said, you might be wishing for those nickels back

Plaintiff

Some home shopping; your fridge is into hip replacement. This
word bubble doesn't work as well as the old one. Criss is suing
cross. These young people memorize transparencies. Her pink
zebra wallet was a fly in the sky of Zion. All roads to the airport are

littered with printing presses. And you see how businesses creep
me. Eyelashes lie like crapped boomerangs on the debit card
receipt. I heard the human race is losing its sensitivity to
thickness. I heard our ancestors threw a party for film processing.
And how did chopped liver become a measure of malignance?
Ever since the aerosol; ever since gunpowder; ever since Eden
Vomitapple took her flugelhorn and quit the quartet? I never loved
life as much as in this instant, especially since Copernicus and
Galileo were though of as opticians

Quid Pogrom

A carrot is a carrot, Chekhov said. Let me whack you with the stick.
Dear The Bushes, a carrot is an origami fist. The top-down breed
with their contraindications readied for sale as kitschy trinkets. The
teacup pinky crick set to spit a deadly venom. All infinitives (those
princeliest syntactic bits) were found the morning after, split. And it

turned out my indignance was behind the microwave, and trucked
in to make the Joint Chief feel adored, and weirdly everywhere like
God's P.R. The proof is in the bowl of Total. With 10% high on
prime rib, Americans are only divisible by themselves and one.
The George W. Bush monument proved to be a wishing well of
2000 year 2000 pennies, with the low relief rubbed off (and barely
a trickle). What's next, civil rights vouchers? I'll vouch for national

morning sickness facing the front page. Our f-ing anthem is about
a flag, how is it we're standardless?

Lake Merlin from *Hike*

Purple Fleabane, Common Harebell, Double Bladder Pod,
Chokecherry, Yellow Dryad, gravity entirely
Merlin was a numbnuts, it's
nature's way of backing the truck up to the loading dock
and rolling off to Jasper with flats of irregular 'picturesque'.
No tourist ever choked on a surveyor's baton,
though the collage of total cheek flesh against
jilted geology makes a museumworthy contrary-to-fact.
Merlin smiled while the unicorns had
very rough sex with a set of granite pinnacles.
Everyone's bodies tattooed "hardly"
The minutes ticking. The ticks minuetting.
Ecotouricide for the however-heeled.
Distant forest fires throw a polarizing filter
over fields of Pearly Everlasting

Buck Downs

from *A Draft of XXX New Personal Problems*

New Personal Problem XVII
    (too much dairy

transnational van
guard smacks of foggy
business writing every
3D commercial. clocks
occlude progress isn't
the point it seemed to
be. etherised on a
kitchen counter it is not
the time to knock it off
all nite & define what is
invisible on the new property.
Riverbend I now sold out.
Blueridge I now selling under.

New Personal Problem XXIX
    (William Shatner

clinical breast-exam
that doubles as fore
play, that there is always
a doubling under. there is
not a lack of understanding,
but a surplus; plunging on
the point at once and for all
it's work as per usual, with a
gasp in take and a little plunge
and pause like it does, after
a hesitation and then it ends.
then there isn't any escape
from release, then, clean for ten
years, that bothers me, that

scares me. How did that make
you feel? Good. Pleroma
of pure light, formless truth
of dissolution in the presence
of an authority a very soft
feature of the landscape.

New Personal Problem XIX
  (Bad Publicity

3+ scotch photography
nightmares stucco friday on
monday like music that doesn't
come from anywhere but here it
comes again, cramped in
the center of the corner, some
where with the hired help out
of bounds; any more specific
and the words begin to extrude
excess self-determination
like shame folded in the etym
ology of pudenda or plain
old vanilla douche doubling
over its own use and intention
(see How to Do Things With Words,
p. 72, et seq.) and it makes my
girl go duh like that shit causes
cancer and so they decided
they got to unload the rest so
we got it on sale.

New Personal Problem XXXII
    (Real-Life Test

Seven a.m. of a Friday night
that's what I'm meaning
when I point Afrosaxon
lack of anything to do w/money
or I'm not Your Old Dixie
Any more. a pocketful
of the bar and grill and
and the life that pulls you
in and then you live there.
end of another long streak
I had thought I would say nothing
or next to nothing but it was mostly
I was just not returning any
phonecalls. somebody
tried to recruit me but
they didn't try long enough
is all. I have gone quite a ways
to get this case of the "shakes",
and now I want to go there again.

Eileen Myles

Inauguration Day

It's snowing in New York
today. I think
of the innocence
of each flake
as it moves through
the sky—Watch it
2001-like, like the universe

wearing its clothes.
If I look close
it's a little flake dying.
I sit in a tarmac
dog-run, a triangular
crotch of real estate,
11th Ave. & 39th
in New York.
Little flake you are
just like me:
born in the clouds in
such innocence, staggering with
your friends in the sky
angels, really, little
voters pushed by the wind
past the Remco building
facing the Lincoln tunnel
the skid of tires on
mildly winter day.
My dog is haunted by your trust
the ceaseless and extravagant dumping
of snow in New York.
Good luck?—is it good luck
to vote, one poem aiming

directly for my eye
but on it's on my sweater
now. America!
If the heavens can dump
this heap of frosty feathers
on us, a reprieve
it seems, a bowl
of beauty for the day.
Cold flowers sent by
December 22 to Jan. 20th,
the months shaking hands,
or me a poet & a Democrat
standing here—who is
this man? You do know
snow—before it falls &
disintegrates, this feathery
hope. You know America.
Growing up to be a voter,
alone we each enter the
sky of history—
(those who were allowed!)
erratic & random it seems
& this is the snow that
just won't last,
the light and watery
see-through kind
but also gorgeous and meaningful kind,
it gives me time
to think, to vote
for the future
of everyone, there is no dictatorship
of the skies
today's weather will end & change
the snow is not human
I am, you cannot insult
Me. I hold this sense of awe.

Rosemarie Trockel: Metamorphoses and Mutations

February 27, 2001

Jennifer Moxley
Marjorie Welish
Tina Darragh

This reading pursued parallels in contemporary writing to Rosemarie Trockel's rich and idiosyncratic use of the tropes of metamorphosis and mutation. Rather than changing things, Trockel often seems to be projecting herself into them, loading objects with a quality and quantity of self and watching what these things will and will not accept. In her "Hope" series, for instance, the face of an ape becomes at once a real bearer of gestural emotion and an almost impossible screen on which we seem to project such emotion, since it must be sought—across species—in the most foreign of languages imaginable. The hope we attribute to the ape, the hope we have of understanding it, and the hope we presume the artist has of somehow representing it, of aping it, all collapse into a complex of meta-mimetic meanings. If Trockel does not see a smooth appropriation of such guises as the ape, the fairy tale character, the movie star, or the ordinary person in the pose of a movie star, neither does she see, simply, an ironic gap between the positions of viewer and viewed—a complete failure of comprehension caused by ridiculous desires. Her work seems instead to explore a kind of hybrid state in which she simultaneously affirms likeness and identification and destabilizes their bases.

One of Jennifer Moxley's central concerns is to develop a new definition of lyricism. This interest emerged at a time when lyric's opposite in one sense—the book based on series or conceived as a single project—had become a kind of de facto mode within the avant-garde, from Zukofsky to Language writing. Given this, Moxley's way of situating her work, not merely her poetry itself, has been pursued with the force of an exemplary imaginative act. Her tonal distance from much contemporary poetry reads as a marker of some special alterity—not escapist, but negative in the most wide-ranging, and ultimately challenging, of senses. What emerges in the wake of this act? Most importantly, I think, a new mode of linkage between effects of timelessness, or lyric insulation, and a social world, so that lyric's embedded ambivalences project not merely toward the micro scale of the concrete second persons frequently evoked in lyric but also toward the larger social structures that are evoked and commonly apostrophized in her work. Thus Moxley remotivates elements within the lyric tradition of Dickinson, Keats, Wordsworth, and others as a form of public speaking where a kind of measuredness and elegance argue for not a retreat or a looping back, but a possible future whose seriousness one can read in part through the force of negation necessary for these very same effects.

In a 1959 poem, "For Bob Rauschenberg," Frank O'Hara responds to the artist's work by claiming to "put everything aside / but what is here." O'Hara knew that this discourse of modernist immanence—with its doctrine of exploring the inherent qualities or resources of media and materials—is precisely what Rauschenberg has been charged with abandoning. O'Hara's poem goes on to project a set of contingent, debatable interpretive frameworks onto Rauschenberg's work: sexual history, musical links and poetic genealogies. In so doing, O'Hara annotates a particular "here" in Rauschenberg, giving it a kind of faux-immanence. Marjorie Welish's selected poems—The Annotated "Here"—might be taken to update and expand this project in less ironic terms. Recognizing that any "here" is an iterable, shifting position, Welish, whose "here" is also often in front of a work of art, "annotates" less by compiling a consistent inventory of sense experiences than by articulating a continuous circuit between such experiences and the conventions and logical assumptions that make them seem real. Though Welish's syntax, especially in the early books, evokes the history of lyricism, vortexes frequently open to reveal the endless implications of "ordinary language" as it enters to have its say about a particular "here." It is in this sense that Welish's poetry is simultaneously a projection onto various locations and an account of the groundlessness of such projections.

If Moxley and Welish complicate the process by which poets project onto poetic forms or artworks, in Tina Darragh's writing the formal raw materials on which such projections operate play, perhaps, an even larger role. Many of Darragh's pieces begin as quasi-narrative accounts of a set of linked concepts—something like rogue etymologies or encyclopedia entries. Rogue, at least, in comparison to a would be objective and definitive strain in encyclopedic thought and a conservative perspective that sees earlier meanings as primary in etymology. But like the earlier, more radical encyclopedists (Diderot, in particular), Darragh uses the occasion of cataloging objects and concepts whose histories leave verifiable traces as a structure for improvisation. Darragh is interested not only in the conditions of discovery (how and where, and the effects these have on what and how we know), but also in the material and social form knowledge has in locations where we encounter it. She reads the social space of a particular library back into the books it contains, or the epistemological implications of a reference guide's graphic layout into the genealogy of a concept the guide glosses, or the physical form of an apartment complex as a guide to two neighbors' developing relationship. Darragh's work is in this sense a set of "for instances" in which the histories of concepts and words get appropriated in the context of quotidian life, setting up chains that link institutions of knowledge to lived experience, and positioning Darragh, frequently, as a reader of her own work, exercising a kind of agency in shifting the route of the research as it develops according to unforeseen needs and possibilities. —LS

Jennifer Moxley

Aide-Memoire

for Jeff Clark

Two delicate, almost masculine hands
enter the nest back to back, palms gracefully out
they cup a klatch of woven filaments, vibrant
downy threads, dark brown, which quiver
against the broken lifelines that selfishly
ease them apart. Adamantine memory was never
so cruel, so hungry for knowledge, being by nature
a passive storage, passive and wholly just.
Incredulous as a cat to every gratis revelation
you, the poet, blandish the ear, the same you enter
and tear to shreds in quest of a truth
you scarcely believe, lest in the wake
of some grand farewell, in the melancholy
gutterspout purl accompanying your stealthy
night-walk home the synapses of those lives
whose flesh once graced your pallid hands
invade your discomposure, insisting
on their contradictions, ulterior innocence,
and grace, charting their eccentric orbit
through the vestibule of your brain, and sexual ploy
turn to selfless need and then to love uncritical,
this last at last condemned for being so vainly
artificial, and so embarrassingly naked.
Through the fragile portal you push, and,
heedless of acidic secretions, enter,
the nest is moist and dark, inside its lattice
divine activity glows phosphorescent
on your tongue, unerring truth plays hide and seek
'til the eyes put out their shutters, the rose-petal ears
filter the dust up-turned by the master's boot,
lustful mouth nine times ensilenced in the cave
of a plural belly pulls, outside the contrivance

the tool of wisdom uproots the oracular stump,
down, down in the ganglion trapped
the uppermost wisps of your coarse black hair
present their plea for indulgence, the careworn subject
once cross-examined by your distrust grows nervous
awaiting the curl of your honest kiss
to release her from the oath, and then the words
come crawling out, one hesitant foot at a time,
out from the disorderly thatch, into the light
they come, by fantastic yarns of birth perplexed,
by nature mechanical and law compelled.

The Best American Poetry

> We are not chickadees
> on a limb...
> —William Carlos Williams

Nothing matters that is not made to matter,
and in this indiscriminate climate
thoughts of the future afford small comfort.
The soul, over which no law adjudicates,
takes of its sustenance in simple ways.
As tonight the indifferent merry dancers
look thoughtful and responsive lighting up
the Northern sky, and the morning chickadee,
a reckless bird, delighted by his morsel,
stills sings before the black-husked seed.
In quaint contrast we stand inside this dreadful
state of reason, unable to couch in art,
or grief—that profiteer of solipsism—
the quandary of nerve it takes to daily
actuate the truth, whether for itself alone
or for this year's unscrupulous scaffold.
What difference does it make, when there are those
who speak contemptuous words with joy, as if
convenient nihilism could be transformed

to hearth and home, unfeigned intent discarded
and embraced at will, as laughing fingers
fumble to adjust the "mask of anarchy."
Only in righteous judgement of the old
will new authority be born, whose errors,
once passed into law, will not admit confusion.
Perhaps a lifetime of squirreled dilemmas
does yield a moment of peace, but oh how
lovely to feel, with all our faculties,
that we have chosen—and that the rhetoric works.
There will always be some outskirt missionary,
trapped in a parable of motives, poised
to invent divine purpose, and to the heart
bound by isolation and despair,
the night sky's luminous phenomenon
will look to be all of a piece. But we,
unlike the bird, need not, in the ferment
of small objectives, desert material
purpose, we can direct the equitable
increments, though they provide no guarantee
the outcome shall be just.

Marjorie Welish

from *Textile*

Textile 6

Insofar as

the turnstile within sentences attributed spaces

like illness across thick lulls

and insofar as

sentences apparently exact hard spaces, posthumous definitions,

deficits

auxiliary surfaces in our reading also.

"The rush of pealing bells cries out in the gorges"

has forwarded how things might have been different.

A different thing.

Textile 7

And as in the mind

a gyroscope

through and beyond gossip

"Of what is past, or passing, or to come"

and its corollaries.

And its copyright

as in the estate of "Gates of Hell"

cooling off

original copies.

As posthumous descriptions

the body in dark and light descant

wax met metal

and lost. As he left them as he let them go:
ash let bodies be copied cordially.
["We've met
before."]

We have lived in emphasis
to establish the mettle of nature
for somewhere

literary entities have disembarked.
"Landscapes," they called it.
Culled
because on land
—"That's not a garden, that's a sanatorium for plants"—,
a sanatorium for flowers
in attendance
has found its women's literature.
False positives

"…as a late cultural arrival…"
as, for example, locale
or tanning

even as a reticent reader works through such maneuvers.

Textile 10

A jumper knitted throughout, a sweater's overcoming mimesis

Less

"Chapter 1 has been suspended in a warehouse/of textiles for 1000th of a second"–at once a
sentence and a sentence in a poetics

Lesser

at once a linguistic event and a linguistic event styled after installation.

Least

Impossible work finds hypothetical situations.

Good

Situations impersonating a book, speech acts walking across stage

Better

situation impersonating a boot, speech acts walking across stag

Best

Suspended in a warehouse, a literary campaign

Loudest

suspended in a disused textile factory, textiles and a second literacy campaign
after cultural evisceration.

Louder

A woman removing her jumper (sweater) in a textile factory

Loud

removes a jumper (sweater), then another pulled inside out, says aloud,
"And now, for the retrograde inversion."

Textile 13

Locomotive

What is a portrait?

Locomotive

When is a portrait not a portrait?

When it is locomotive
not physiognomic
insofar as pasturing.
"Tendency of ideas to go over into movement"
Movement
as such.
Movement was used.
Walking along a walk
"as fully as possible."
Walking the walk
Stance? Pavement?
As passage.
As passage to pavement
walking the walk
republished as
"Tendency of ideas to go over into movement.
For these experiments

the subject was given a pencil."
By the people.
Men At Work.
As in the phrase
"working women."

Tina Darragh

"Bunch-Apes Mutation"
    for Rosemarie Trockel

vocal tract anatomy

single "ha"   to   "ha-ha-ha-ha-ha"   to
                                                lip-smacking
                                                superimposed
loose ratio of disconnects

when I hand larger than blind
pure follow is plea

communication not

                    necessary for   tool
behavior

                              much debate
about commonalities
                                        speech and tool
behavior

ained pictures
pend to only scund

          see a better toolkit

volcanic scoria pebble in the naturally-occurring shape of a female
torso

                                                haft

Credit

With the mapping of the human genome called "complete," information is reorganized into huge databases designed to link clinical data to genetic sequences. Items with a direct link—such as research findings on family planning, environmental pollution, managed care administration, and space medicine—are publicly available but "lost in the shuffle."

The origin of a published photo of anti-WTO demonstrators is a mystery. A person's name is printed beside the picture, but when contacted he has no knowledge of it; when recontacted, he says he did not know it had been published, and anyway, it isn't his. The magazine's editors report that the negative has been returned to the person who took the photo, but they can't recall who that is.

The work of medieval anatomist Guido de Vigevano—sixteen drawings with Latin legends—are included as an appendix to the reproduction of eight different editions of the anatomy of Mondino dei Luzzi: Edition A. Carcano, Edition H. de Durantibus, Edition J. de Paucisdrapis, Edition genevoise, Edition H. de Benedictis, Edition A. Blanchard, Edition A. Lotrain et D. Janot, and Edition C. Egenolph (Edition E. Droz, Paris, c. 1926.)

Mass distribution of credit card offers to jobless college students begins in 1972 after market research begun in 1970 indicates that Vietnam-era debt can be recouped, in part, from those protesting the war.

Wire boxes

"By midday, the direct-action turtles met up with about sixty legally protesting turtles who had joined about 50,000 other citizens in a labor parade. Those turtles had received the loudest cheer of the day from the assembled steelworkers, Teamsters, and AFL-CIO rank and file when they entered Memorial Stadium carrying a 20-foot-long inflatable mama turtle." (The Amimal's Agenda, Jan/Feb 2000, p. 10 [on the Sea Turtle Restoration Project's participation in the anti-WTO demonstrations in Seattle, Washington, U.S., December, 1999])

LEAD: Full page ad in the NY Times announces alliance of nearly 200 labor and environmental groups. BODY: WTO dispute panel rules against U.S. law requiring all shrimp sold in U.S. to be caught in nets with sea turtle escape devices, and challenges France's asbestos ban. Steelworkers and forest protection activists initially join forces against Maxxam, Inc's clearcuts of ancient redwoods in Northern California, and its 13 month lockout of Kaiser Aluminum plants in Washington, Ohio, and Louisiana. (Inter Press Service, 10/5/99)

LEAD: India's Industry Minister announces that India will not repeat in Seattle the mistakes made at the Uruguay Round. BODY: The Minister attacks the "eco-imperialism" of rich countries, accusing them of using the issue of environmental degradation as a "Trojan horse" against developing countries. (Agence France Presse, 11/2/99)

LEAD: Press conference at University of Washington introduces Alliance members. BODY: National Lawyers Guild promises to send legal observers to the demonstrations. Representatives from the following groups make statements: Rukus, Global Exchange, Rainforest Action Network, Animal Welfare Institute, and People's Global Action Caravan. Labor union presidents represent the AFL-CIO, Teamsters, Steelworkers, Machinists, and United Auto Workers. (Associated Press State & Local Wire, 11/24/99, PM cycle)

LEAD: Downtown Seattle is a street bazaar of social issues with police in riot gear stationed at major intersections. BODY: A 5:00 AM investigation of a bomb scare at the Convention Center curtails the time available for a symposium of environmental, labor, and other groups presenting their positions to WTO officials. 50,000 anti-WTO activists come to town for "The Battle in Seattle" or "Carnival against Capitalism." Jose Bove, leader of the French Peasants' Confederation, distributes Roquefort cheese outside a McDonald's to demonstrate that the U.S. has banned Roquefort cheese because France won't accept U.S. beef treated with hormones. (Associated Press State & Local Wire, 11/30/99, AM cycle)

LEAD: Protesters and delegates described as Harry Potter characters. BODY: The "principle of discourse" prevails until the "You Know Whos" arrive, another HP reference, this time describing the anarchists. (Knight Ridder/ Tribune News Service, 12/4/99)

LEAD: "It has been a long, dry run for the nation's Repressed Protest Class." BODY: RPC protests too confusing even for an anti-WTO computer programmer, and a graduate student with a "very nice, pseudo-academic life." A "white mostly garden party," the protests aren't linked to civil rights and therefore do not address the issues of the poor. (Knight Ridder/Tribune News Service, 12/5/99)

LEAD: The reporter is surrounded by anti-WTO demonstrators after viewing "Pokemon: The First Movie." BODY: Microsoft is surprisingly not a target of the demonstrators, possibly because of their need for email. Earlier WTO talks in Uruguay were held without fax machines. The poor in developing countries may or may not benefit from WTO policies. (Asahi News Service, 12/6/99)

March 13, 2001

Anselm Berrigan
Jean Day
Lyn Hejinian

This reading explored the metamorphoses and mutations of the fable or fairy tale. Trockel's featured drawings were three kinds of projection: onto fairy tale characters like Pinocchio; onto finger puppets (this time by animals, shown operating them); and, finally, onto movie stars, or ordinary people caught in the poses of movie stars. These last drawings highlighted their generic photographic sources not merely through the presentation of familiar poses, but also through the careful reproduction of blur and distortion, of the degradation of the infinitely reproduced and enlarged image. Thus, the drawing process itself became a way to register distance from the mythic objects of attention, to displace the immediacy of identification into mediating representational conventions.

And it is displacement and mediation that, perhaps, connect Trockel's interest in fables, fairy tales, and myths to that of many contemporary poets. In regard to these three readings, the description of myth and fable I've just given might seem, at first, the least intuitively complete or satisfying when applied to Anselm Berrigan's work. Still, despite variation, Berrigan's writing can often be understood as transforming and deforming mythology, if we hear that word not in the classical sense but in the sense that Roland Barthes gives it, as the fundamental mechanism of ideology, which allows the cultural to seem natural. Berrigan's poetry addresses itself to the overdetermined myths of the poet as bohemian, as revolutionary, and as a heroic character who converts experience into a special kind of currency. It's not that Berrigan is unsympathetic to these roles, but that historical conditions have made those who evoke them unselfconsciously seem stilted. Gliding between idiolects or phrase worlds, Berrigan registers generational, historical shifts that have forever changed the meaning, not merely of the idiolects themselves, but of the poets who would weave them together and understand their cultural role precisely through this weaving. This is in part because corporate lexicons have forever colonized, branded, logoed, and identity-managed vast zones of experience that, just a generation ago, seemed to promise spontaneity and freedom. Considering mythology both at the level of the phrase and of the implied poetic persona, Berrigan could thus be thought to turn a kind of ethical/lingusitic damage management into an art form wherein using humor and verbal invention to point to evaporating possibilities builds others.

Jean Day's poetry is frequently associated with a critique and transformation of the lyric "I." What is less commonly noticed, and what might link her in this context to Trockel, is her exploration of the spatial and geographical implications of fables and myths, especially national ones. In Day's most recent book, The Literal World, the drama of American westward expansion, with all of its linguistic formulations and rationalizations, merges with the drama of familial expansion in the present. One function of the fable or myth, especially in the national context, is to explain a complex present, with its multiple lines of causality, as an example of an atemporal, or an ahistorical, morality. In Day's work, fairy tale and fable operate in almost the opposite way: unconscious rationalizations of the status quo bubble up into and complicate the present, projecting it back into the muddy past. This accounts in part for the fluidity of Day's "I" (its picaresque adventures, displacements, expansions and contractions), since geography in her writing contains partially buried ideological structures that, suddenly emerging from the literal surface of the world, refuse to remain past or submerged. These obstacles are literal for Day in the sense that they are inescapable features of everyday geography.

Lyn Hejinian's exploration of the fable and fairy tale in books such as A Border Comedy and The Traveler and the Hill comes out of her larger interest in epistemology. One way to think of the fable is as having a syllogistic, three-part structure, as constituting a tiny epistemological system that allows one to draw conclusions from a mini-narrative: there was once an X; Y happened; this means Z—context, event, conclusion. Why this specific logical structure seems persuasive is a question Hejinian has explored, often quite hilariously, by deforming fables and fairy tales so that the neat, section-to-section fit opens into a world of flux and contingency, with potential knowledge arriving at each phase but never sitting in its assigned seat: Y does not follow from X, or follows from an arbitrary, secondary element; the conclusion Z seems parachuted from another story. And though these gaps and displacements are, first of all, funny, they also point to the rhetorical and institutional structures that allow what we might call knowledge effects. This exploration of edges and cracks within fairy tales can be seen as a component of Hejinian's larger concern with borders, especially the borders between abstract ideas and examples—between, on the one hand, the comparatively timeless world of principles, theories, morals, and, on the other, the more time-bound, sense-experience-based world of examples and anecdotes. As the philosophers remind us, everything depends upon the seam between these. It is precisely this seam that is the most active and inventive border in Hejinian's writing. —LS

Anselm Berrigan
from *Zero Star Hotel*

Them—from over there
A beak is better
Than a Swiss Army
Knife. Radioactive
Pellets protect
The mayor's prostate
We and it advance
The Shat is very good
Knows about "The Ribbon"
dies twice

lampposts jostling
vicinities taller than
all Sam's life, Livre
de Brouillon, thought
balloon blur, fill them
with outdated one-armed
robots wearing jade
chokers and amber
elephant pendants in
the tub, cookie soap

Joppy retains middle-
Weight belt, Devils
Lose in overtime
Aphorisms are for
Jerks, the toner
Tasted like Mongolian
Beef, somewhere's
Cranium could be
Heard muttering
Through a commission

boy bat bats boy
a welcoming display
tainted water glug
glugs down throat
awkward places
and other phrases
product one thinks
this fluidity between
abstraction and talk
is a portal to a portal

Through a brick wall
Under Penn Station
Up to the Bronx
To The World of
Darkness. Largest
Living rodent zoos
My cosmic bring
Make that largest
Species of. Our
Greying budget

priorities. Would
the landlord ever
fix the front door?
if I give him copies
of my poems will
he understand me?
the happening skips
goodbye quarter
and what but the wash
to go get

But not the trad-future
My health and economy
About color patterns
Reflecting something made
There, smoke stunk
All my sleeves hang
Into an add-on closet
Steak, totally staring
Carvers do not faces
But I'll tell you this

Dream Pig speaks:
"Let's get the flock
Out of the United
States." Pdiddle
As brain state
Can't afford replace-
Ment light. Six
Instances of non-
Violent resistance:
Uh, uh, uh, uh, um, uh

Kicking selves and in
Exchange I gave you
Such a heart, a well
Armed feeling mind
Hey hey you you
The medicine we can't
Afford to change
The way we'll be
Clairvoyance is easy
That we isn't me

a tiger, a hornbill
a sea lion. Dan:
a chameleon, the
disheveled brown
bird of yesterday
and something else
Eddie: giraffe, killer
whale. Bon: elephant
lynx, something. Dream
traveling companions

to be admitted to Death
Cube, in acid-etched
metal, at a bar
of artfully corroded
steel, insectoid
mandibles moving
forward into brown
light, walls unevenly
transparent, flat
and doll-like

lashing out at everyone
as a personal quality
has been making me
difficult to be around
completely reinhabited
though the explanation
is an endeavor unto
itself, I tend to want
information, no right
line wants to be here

Must make sure teaching
Doesn't destroy me
Starting with commuter
Discount orange zesty
Cherry burst and
That's the idea
You keep the hair
That you have
It's stronger
Than heredity

the big ten looks
terrible, jogger types
every proposition
braced on an emergency
animal rescue story:
what if we see an animal
in trouble? do what
you can to get
somewhere safe
then page me

Thus it is stronger
Than it is in
Morphoplasticism
I feel compelled
To admit that such
A clarification
Has led me with
Regard to the comp-
Licated progress
Of taking sides

passing through
several phases
gradually eliminated
descriptive elements
like his bleeding
necklace, and beans
do they really think
Silver may still be
sitting in his cage
waiting for us?

Silver was not
The only bird
Scaling the scaffolding
In a geometric
Progression
While cutting class
Ever had the price
Stamp come down
On your head
A photo can stomach it

the shopkeeper knew
I only bought
to legitimize our
entry into his store
while my friends
plundered the aisles
divorced from
the natural world
and formal code
kleptos in progress

Universality ignores aliens
I never sound that
Is how we have been
Accumulated drip stains
Services honestly, simply
Our direction has been
Absolutely forerunning
Slowed to foretrotting
Okapis on bivouac lane
View by dollar van

Staring at me, and
Only I ever seem to
See it. Greg may
No longer believe
The mouse is real
But, perhaps, a fig
Newton of my eviction
And his. Green ceiling
Goodbye forever
C-I-L the landlord

Parking lot spring-joy
In an alternate kite
Blows wig across
The promenade, deck
Patio, foyer, red cobra
Exhibit, the alligator
Snapping butterfly
Wing of powdered
Death buffet with
Chlorinated bath

that the real dying
took place between
surfaces, this drowned
man in a poem insists
through witness digging
by the shoreline
one experiences
a subjective beatdown
back home this mouse
was sitting on my bed

all year long I've been
trying to get the tone
wrong and winding
up forward, I'm way
ahead of my debts
headlights tumble
off the road, only
the steering wheel
survived, furry legs
race into restroom

what if I wake up
with the mouse in bed?
why has it come into
my life? I have no food
or time to bond, and
am in a state of forced
departure, cruel human
life awaits my future
in kinds of ballads and
drool called English, mouse

Jean Day

from *Sixteen Lucky Dreams (Epical Pictures)*

One (Meter)

"Meanwhile in our booth

even a little finger could dream of a crowd

nostalgic and sad like two orioles

attacking one small subaltern

dragonfly off duty on the hand of a former

farmer a dictator reformed

now to simple fusion obstreperous

and genetic a cloud spills perilous

over yellow a dress

sent from pantlegs in exile

hayseeds and all it begins with a dactyl

or aftershock to look up.

But the sky is no place for data."

So saying, the dream is a remake.

Two (Gem)

Inside the speech meter perked

officially a circus dream and prime

stumbling like the shy elephants

who strode towering to our town in summer

for the tonic. In that new world or tent

it was said by speech

one adopts all poses apple-green

like skin not a part but a condition

external to matter (love) whose ends

make awesome the sky (or weather; the near and far sides

of its discontinued monument)

attached to which an elephant

(now a cow)

stands by a filament

docile for the dawn and a great favorite.

Three (Visit)

"Galloping on a mettlesome stallion the visitor

comes home on the rain

falls from the sun just to be fair

to the diligent proofreader of an unusual shade—

blue behind an oxidized door where

individuals trade parts scribbling "Twas

ever thus' in clownish script

on the blank slates

of each other's backs. There

Magnanimous Despair arrives

great in the ear a verse

fitted with birds, tears, oranges, undergarments, the starchy

sky a heaving sun—all reasons

to hurl the writing instrument away

as the same water travels up and down the crystal tube

day after day."

Four (Turning Blue)

What strange rain recurs then

silhouetted in mid-air

falls on the last night of a demon

decoy one foot in the air who

adjusting her ankle as a fragment of the beat

disappears begins "What drop

convinces amid scenes of contagious

shooting? Penetrates the tongue and rests there

before anyone can explain

pneuma to us

arrows rain, crumbs legion

I and everyone

set up for instruction?"

Lyn Hejinian

from *The Little Book of A Thousand Eyes*

The bed is made of sentences which present themselves as what they are
Some soft, some hardly logical, some broken off
Sentences granting freedom to memories and sights

Then is freedom about love?
Bare, and clumsily impossible?
Our tendernesses give us sentences about our mistakes
Our sentiments go on as described
The ones that answer when we ask someone who has mumbled to say what he or she has
      said again
In bed I said I liked the flowing of the air in the cold of night
Such sentences are made to aid the senses

Tonight itself will be made—it's already getting dark
I'm not afraid to look nor afraid to be seen in the dark
Is there a spectral sentence? a spectator one?
Is it autobiographical?
No–the yearning inherent in the use of any sentence makes it mean far more than "we
      are here"

Because we are not innocent of our sentences we go to bed
The bed shows with utter clarity how sentences in saying something make something
Sentences in bed are not describers, they are instigators

***

The picture appears suddenly in its entirety
It begins nowhere, and I'm faced with it
I'm against the wall opposite it facing an audience and replying to the many objections
       that the audience is lodging against existentialism
The picture raises no such objections, being ridiculous in its own right
It is there by virtue of a mere fluke with silent placidity
The picture is of a cow then?

I have to turn away

A cow?
Then?
There's a cow on a board?
Board, certainly, but no cow, and we term that a picture?

That it's of a cow rather than a battle is not a disappointment

I never see cows in order

I neglect to do battle willingly out of cowardice

I'm avaricious, I want the picture

I would settle for a picture of the picture

I am no Shostakovich

The picture begins
There are no mistakes in it but it is of mistakes and nervousness and disappointment
There is a knife in it
There are knocks, there's a sequence of loud knocks

***

Ooooh, ooooooh, ooooh, says the voice of a girl:

I've been attacked by owls,
by owls with towels,
I've been attacked
by snakes with rakes.

It is just this kind of ridiculous language, banal but lacking even banality's pretense at relevance and sense, that I hear in my sleep; I wake, feeling irritable and depressed.

***

The world is between tips
We say so to know
We go to look over or out to its pivot, to its wobble and drift
· Terrible
We are leaving
There's nothing to come to there but transformation and tint
Seductions
So we can't be repeating
What one knows in this state can't be known in another
Time matches nothing

A person circles sleeps to pines or tides in entered light
Thousands depend on one
Repeated
And all that's repeated is mediated
Thought
The order is such that it situates
At the farthest extent of a scene are its reachings
Night life is search of its kind
Reach
A gesture not of things but of crevice, preface, prelude
I imagine without standpoint, poised at loss point
At pole
And the horizon doesn't hold there
Its gaping point of contact spreads the latitudes
The pole is interminable, coming and going to arrive
It shares the mobility of an oblivion I want to witness

Human curiosity contradicts the human will to believe
But what's the denial of solving
It is a happiness to wonder
Night visions rhyme
And because of their obscurity they seem uncanny
They undertake that more than mathematical spreading of pattern that seems to be the
    root of all beauty
It lets us mock and destroy the utterly complete
With night thoughts like these, are we not logicians

Is the sleeper leaning to make contact with reality?
Everything is scattered beyond the face
Detached
But persons have their immortality to sacrifice—and why stop?

***

The 23rd night was very dark.
It was cold.
My eyes were drawn to the window.

I thought I saw a turtledove nesting on a waffle
Then I saw it was a rat doing something awful
But anarchy doesn't bother me now any more than it used to

I thought I saw a woman writing verses on a bottle
Then I saw it was a foot stepping on the throttle
But naturally freedom can be understood in many different ways

I thought I saw a fireman hosing down some straw
Then I saw it was a horse grazing in a draw
But it's always the case that in their struggle to survive, the animate must be aided

I thought I saw a rhubarb pie sitting on the stove
Then I saw it was the tide receding from a cove
But although I have strong emotions when I watch a movie, jealousy is never one
      of them.

I thought I saw a bicyclist racing down the road
Then I saw it was a note, a message still in code
But sense is always either being raised to or lowered from the sky

I thought I saw a gourmet chef smear himself with cream
Then I saw it was myself just entering a dream
But we all know that the imagination when left to itself will brave anything

Between Street
and Mirror:
The Drawings of
James Ensor

May 22, 2001

Kevin Davies
Renee Gladman
Lisa Robertson

This reading projected two trajectories into contemporary writing from the drawings of the Belgian Expressionist James Ensor (1860–1949), who in his twenties began not merely to revise his earlier work but, in a sense, to parody it—unsettling his previous relation to the genres of the still life and the portrait. It's almost as if, in Ensor's reading of his own previous work, the still life and the portrait implied an overly neat emotional economy—a set of values he could no longer endorse. Whereas the Danish painter Asger Jorn would, in the 1950s, seek out other people's genre paintings (bought in thrift stores and at fairs) in order to perform this same operation (actually painting them over while leaving traces of the earlier moment, now hopelessly scarred, reframed, or diluted), Ensor subjected his own work to this process. The result was not merely generic hybridity, which is common enough both in art and writing, but a more parasitic relationship to genre, one that could only be acted out in time: the values associated with a genre were allowed to enter the world, exist for a period, and then underwent radical negation—but a negation that is also a transformation. If this is one pole of Ensor's work, another, just as compelling and relevant to contemporary writing, is an extreme, often disturbing relationship to the genre of the caricature, a genre in which representational instrumentality—the reduction of mimesis to a seamless system of socially coded signs—might turn against itself. Obviously the reduction of identity to a graphic shorthand carries an oppressive threat. Still, one of the progressive possibilities of the caricature is to use these visual signs of social role as a way to explore the conditions and conventions that allow for the genre's legibility.

The picture of the social world we get in Ensor's 1889 drawing Doctrinaire Nourishment *(1889), which shows several priests, a businessman, a king, and a general shitting into the faces of an eager crowd below might provide an analog for one of the central projects in Kevin Davies's most recent book,* Comp.*—to explore the linguistic forms and social processes by which efficient, docile human subjects are composed. As with Ensor, this ranges in Davies from what is actually said to what is somehow implicit: "I love the look of humans when they sit or stand still and when they move around. / I love the look of them looking back and barking arbitrary commands, which I obey." If caricature in the nineteenth century provided one way, graphically, to imagine the literalization, the making concrete, of repressive ideological structures, Davies's work explores the phrase as a similar tool. What is less familiar to viewers of caricature, though, is the broad range of possible authorial and subject positions we*

encounter in one of Davies's poems. In fact, the rapid movement between formal struc-
tures in a poem like "Karnal Bunt" in Comp. *can be taken as an analogy for both*
shifting subject positions that teach us where we stand—"You pictured it you bought
it. You burnt it down you gotta sweep it up"—and for a kind of global frustration,
even rage, at learning our position, which motivates the poem as a whole, intention-
ally conflating world historical and subjective scales: "the completion of modernity, the
washing up, the beers after." Davies's social humor forces us not merely to picture the
troubling and unpicturable processes at work, but to live with them, since we already are.

Renee Gladman's first two books, both in prose, use an authorial first person that
formulates sentences to and about a range of second persons as a way to reinvent
the roles available within social groups. But Gladman's prose is not a sociology or
political theory that offers itself to the future; rather, it suggests that it is already, in
itself, an embodiment of the experimental epistemology and social theory she develops.
In The State, *Gladman performs an inversion of this previous project (from utopia*
to dystopia) by describing the consciousness of a political prisoner who cannot entirely
separate her thoughts from the various truth serums and torture techniques forced
upon her by her captors. And yet rather than a work about the psychology of torture, or
the inexorable expansion of the state, Gladman's elegant and paradoxically autono-
mous sentences give The State *a revolutionary vigor, as though Che were channeling*
Descartes in Guantanamo.

Lisa Robertson's writing positions a deformation of two literary genres—the eclogue
and the epic—as the frame through which transformations of the social become visible
and possible: "if Virgil has taught me anything," writes Robertson, "it's that authority
is just a rhetoric or style which has asserted the phantom permanency of a context."
This phantom permanency, with its authority located in the context-building ef-
fect of genre, is what we see Ensor defacing with graffiti in his hybrid drawings. For
Robertson, graffiti on the big time literary genres operates in two seemingly opposite
ways: on the one hand, through a kind of extreme sound patterning (euphony turned
to eleven), which we are offered as an uncontainable excess that parasitically works
its way back toward the foundational status of "beauty" in understandings of the
literary; on the other, through shifts in registers of address that, still sonically pleasant

most of the time, introduce statements about the very construction of genre (like the one about Virgil quoted above) that embarrass and reframe the proceedings, linking genre's authoritative parceling and slicing to the interested maintenance of social and gender divisions, inside and outside the literary sphere. But what separates Robertson from others who have similarly critiqued the social functions of genre is the extent to which her writing proposes a thorough reoccupation rather than a distanced critique, as though real transformation could only be immanent. —LS

Kevin Davies
from *The Golden Age of Paraphernalia*

Cold snap - old shoes.

Something they put in the gas
to make the air better
has made the water worse.
Tumours in rats.

The mayor's city is almost up to code

    aside from the asbestos grade schools and rotting projects
    of a previous order, public. July 15, 1999.

        *

someone hands another a torn ticket
both face it puzzled
eyes as though poked

        *

The same shoes.

        *

Places arrived at only by people with cars
and those who are already there.
What happens if one pulls this lever?

        *

The same hill, different shoes.
Repeat. The same hill,
different shoes. A different hill.

                    *

You're always having that extreme thought
in relation to an audience,
you know.

                    *

If it isn't sex
why are we thinking about it?

Our prosimian ancestors
less than one ounce,
ankles smaller than rice grains.
Scooped up and eaten by owls.
Having just done the wild thing.

If it isn't food
why are we thinking about it?

                    *

A finger, an entire arm
pointing to a moon
in a puddle
in a mirror-
say something.

                    *

Exact middle of this partnership we live with
I almost woke up. "High-definition television? These fuzzy things?"

*

parodies of the teachable moment

If it looks like a poem, it's a restraining order.

You'd have to cut the wall in half to consult the real calendar.

The email sublime - live turtles
in the fibre optics, swimming towards Hull.

*

So, what kind of artist were you
before you became the worker you are now?

*

The neighbour cat has elaborate
aesthetic responses to weather.
I would stake Robert Creeley's life on such assumptions.

*

The urban walker relives this
England, playing tricks, enduring revision. Older,
I keep forgetting what I've watched.

The wind's blowing out.
Open stance an inch.
Pull.

What I'm looking for in a video,
late at night, drinking,
is the opposite of identification,
the negation of catharsis,
plus lots of landscape.

My tutees read Beowulf in rages.
That pitch was taken.
Took. Earlier,

Reznikoff pauses on a bridge,
reworking an image in history,
stoned.

Mansion, yacht, and high-powered friends.
I woke yet again in a parking lot with graffiti on my ass.
Remarks are literature.

Renee Gladman
from *The State*

Whether this is a dream in which I've been captured or whether I've been captured and made to think I'm in a dream, I cannot figure. In one moment, the scenery is indistinguishable from that which I am accustomed to: I sit at this table, I lay my hands on its surface. But in the next moment, I can't feel my hands and this table pushes against me. I sense the presence of others. At times, I see them.

The last thing I remember doing before I could no longer discern reality proper was preparing for a get-together with a few top-ranked members of our group. We were celebrating the success of our latest direct action, the group's most radical plan to date. It involved Alonso, Lomarlo, and myself posing as corporate CEOs at the *Conference for Global Infiltration*, a weekend symposium for the world's richest businessmen. As participants, we had complete access to all kinds of financial databases into which we planted numerous...now how much should I say not knowing my predicament, not knowing if these events, which I am so compelled to relay right now, will be used against me? I can imagine nothing worse than being on trial and having my defense corrupted by my own confession—and not even a true confession, because I am innocent.

I will tell anyone who asks that for the past few weeks I have done nothing but wake and sleep. I have not left the house; I have not made any phone calls. I am in the same clothes and, except when dreaming, in the same mood. To the first person who asks, I will disclose the details of my full name, my place of birth, my age, and sun sign. I have nothing to hide. All I have done is sit at this table awaiting the group, whom I have not seen in days.

Conversely, though, I am not against the possibility that I am dreaming. In a way, that reality would be what I always wanted. I have never been a good dreamer, so if true, I could say I've transcended my usual monotony. I would have proof of my subconscious. However, there is some clue in the body. If I had been sitting at my table and, after hours of contemplation, fell asleep and into this imaginary world, then my body should, in a crucial sense, be out of time. So why is my hair growing? And why do I think about hunger? Whoever has captured me and is playing this inhuman trick is not the smartest of criminals. If you want a person to believe that he is dreaming, when in fact he is locked to a chair on drugs, you have to remove his body from time. You have to feed him to keep his mind off his body. Or do you? I can't figure out which is the right indicator of being in time: feeling hungry or satiated. But I do know there is a discrepancy.

—I think I said that last part out loud because something has swung and bounced off my face, and now I am on the floor. I am on my back, looking at the ceiling, which is covered in wires and mirrors and loaves of bread. Legs of pants with militaric creases surround me; congealed body water falls on my cheeks and slides into my ears. I hear a music-like screeching, an Italian opera, then luminousless silence.

—A moment later, I'm feeling particularly at home, but I remember what has just happened to me. I look at my hands, trying to place the last encounter in a circuit of time, and fan myself to lessen the impact of my ineptitude. When I turn my head and see someone I know at the other end of the table, I lose confidence that this is my dinning room. Even though I know him, he does not act as though he's my guest. In fact, someone is sitting in front of him. I watch him move his mouth while the other person scribbles frantically across a page. The synchronicity of their action reminds me of factory machines. What, in itself, is so innocent—speech or penmanship—reeks of evil in this room. I don't think my friend knows where he is. His mouth moves incessantly, but his manner is not his own. What did they do to him? Seeing him violated in this way infuriates me. Soon I will have to smash my fist through the table—that is, if my arms are free. But I bet this is what they want. I'll beat my fists against the unyielding wood, and by that act of defiance, incriminate myself. What good is evidence, though, when it is gathered in a non-existent place? If I could understand that parallelism, then I would know how to act.

I haven't said anything for a while because I've been struggling against subjugation: I'm in a dank room, surrounded by more pleats. The drugs they forced on me have seized power over my nervous and muscular systems, making me want to talk and reveal my true emotions. I have been invaded and am almost occupied through the core. As the chemical levels uninhibiting me increase, I can no longer postpone the moment. I begin, with uncharacteristic honesty:

A day last fall, I set out to take a walk across a bridge. Fallen leaves, still brown and gold, ran along its sides. I studied the leaves because I thought there was something representative in them. I am always looking for analogueies, thinking that eventually I will stumble upon an image that will change the face of the world. It would stand in for those words that continuously elude me. I watched leaves land and curl against each other. When I reached the center of the bridge, I heard laughter from below. I was not used to laughter so, out of profound interest, I ran to the edge to see. I admit I was startled by the source. There was a group, a number of persons clad in river colors. They had bags and weapons when they looked and called to me. Did I know them? When they reached me, they spoke in grave tones of a difficult yet calculated mission. There were certain things they thought I could do. The leader, a woman, held open a suitcase inside of which lay apparent plans. From beneath the pile of papers, she withdrew a contraption that resembled a circuit board. She held it out to me and spoke in words that were just barely foreign. The others of her group had left us and were performing gymnastics near the wall of the bridge. She wanted me to take the mechanism from her and put it in the crevice of the wall. I had left the house to take a walk that day—did I say that already? Yes, perhaps they had mistaken me. I admit that I fell in with them. The leader placed the switch in my hand and added more of her alien tongue. Though I conceded to slip the switch into the crevice, nothing happened to the bridge. In fact, I took that same walk across the bridge over the next eight days, having forgotten about that experience. The day the bridge blew, I was east of the city.

—I think I went on speaking for hours, talking beyond the effects of the drugs, as though welcomed by the presence of someone listening. Though as I say that I realize that it too may be a consequence of the drugs. I don't know all of what I told, but for a while, it felt good. Now, however the uncertainty and resentment is returning. I wonder why I should say anything more, especially if it's true that I'm dreaming. —I am struck by the ingenuity of this idea. If I were to say aloud something like "I'm done speaking," there would have to be a response: in answering me, my captors will have to divulge the right reality. If they talk then I know that I'm not dreaming, that I'm locked up somewhere on drugs. No, if they talk…Wait! I lost the relation again. Every time I feel certain that I have devised a way of procuring from my captors or conversely from my imagination which world I'm in, the path that I took to get there fails to maintain its shape. I reach for it and see it multiply itself by two, and as soon as I see that, it grows or lessens in dimension. The idea that I thought would save me dissipates mercilessly.

Some talking has awakened me; there is absolute darkness in this place and no smell. I can't even sense the presence of the inanimate—a table or chair would orient me—I believe I'm utterly alone, so prior to existence that dust has had no time to form. However, I am certain of that voice speaking. It repeats the same passage, though varies the tone for effect. I am unaware of the identity and whereabouts of the supposed receiver of these words. Though I hear the words, they are not directed at me. I would have no idea how to answer such questions.

A hand slams against a surface, a light comes on, my insides respond as though set to a timer, and I begin talking. Time passes, then I stop talking. The man in front of me, who was not there a moment ago, nods his head, apparently an encouragement to go on. Unfortunately, I have lost the inclination. I am exhausted and there is a smudge blocking my peripheral vision. I want to ask my interlocutor what it is. But if he says nothing, I will be disappointed. I ask. He says nothing. I am disappointed. Moreso, I want to pull out my hair now that I've become aware of the smudge, which is practically on top of me, in the way of bugs. I grab for my hair, but—as if I were deeply dreaming—I am unable to isolate the specificity of my hands from the general density I presume to be my body.

The sound of a crash startles me. I turn my head. My friend has fallen, still in his chair, to the floor, surrounded by the captors. They use the uniformity of their dress to intimidate him. Or is it me who is intimidated by the sight of them, huddled in tan and hunched over, dropping globs of spit onto his face? He looks up, past these men and stares without arrest at the ceiling. At first, I am perplexed by his easy fixation. Then I remember the suspended loaves of bread. I begin yelling, but am forced to stop when one of the pants begins to kick me. I'm on my back, with only my eyes free to move. And spit stings them. The bread looks delectable. Every impulse in my body tells me I want it. I scream, and then am kicked until I stop screaming, which coincides with coming to at this table.

Lisa Robertson
from *The Men*

I'm making a record of the men as I know them, their hours and their currencies
and their simple sex. I'll be their glamorous thing and then I won't. Their coats
are casual, they are entirely casual in their stance and I paste my record up.

When a man rides with a demon, when he transmits and snags, when a man feels
his psyche work all over america in its humble way, when he has no obligation,
when he marches on, when a man marches on, when he has hideous knowledge
and he marches with it in the burnt grass, when men believed so many things,
when a man's name is sewn in the label of my coat, when the men's cocks face out
to sea, lovely

And I thank them.
Their theory is what people think.

Now I have this urgency and no patrons.

No man can censure
No man can judge
No man knows.
Yet is every man observed by any man.
I perceive every man.
There is no man that apprehends and no
Man that so nearly apprehends.
To multiply in men
God loves man
Thus one man cuts through another with a clean edge.
It is like a man, this one fabric
Of man. But men's minds also find no rest. With all men
There is no man. There is no man's mind.
The man without pity lives in me.
There is no man alone because every man is the world. Men that look

Sometimes do speak. Every man truly
Positions men. Decadently I withdraw their landscape.
Thus I perceive a man. The twelfth part of man is the crooked piece of man.
I find no rest in any
Thereby becoming the unstable element.
In brief, I am content.

From a dream and the conformity to law
Apart from my thoughts
They rouse from their organic slumber
To present themselves to my senses
With their even gaze.
I have nothing left for them but the absolute tiredness of the series.
I speak of men as they appear to me
Not of men in themselves
I have only experience
And no knowledge.

In experience and for experience only
For the sake of experience they are men.
They have substance for experience only.
I distinguish them from a dream.
This is therefore a decisive experiment.
I know more than this but I can't reach it
And real pain crowds my real head
In the representation.
Their earth is so little
We cannot attribute freedom to the men.

Awful sighs that never end I venture from my style
Against style
As birds, grass, evening
Temporarily boy-like
To make the thing intelligible.
The same actions are free
That caption determination
Such as awful sighs that never end
In cinema
In fact
This is all I require—
That in the literal transparency
I see the dark of evening
I see the night of the green woods tomorrow
I see animate and waiting a rich shore
That's neither love nor notes, freedom nor reason, story nor lyric, boredom
nor strings, Albertine.

June 26, 2001

Adam DeGraff
Ange Mlinko
Jackson Mac Low

Circling back on Ensor's project of unsettling the familiar emotional tones of genre painting, and his cultivation of a kind of materialism, this reading presented the works of two younger writers—Ange Mlinko and Adam DeGraff—in relation to Jackson Mac Low, who began writing in the late 1930s, and was later associated with Fluxus. More recently, he has been influential for both New York School and Language writers. The question of tone also emerges in Ensor's quite amazing prose. To a friend putting together an exhibition of Ensor's, the painter writes: "Who is taking part and what have they done? What are the rooms like and what is the circulation? I don't know anything and so I wait, anxious and uncertain, bristling and defiant... brimming with gall, cloven-footed, my tattered heart fed with the venom of others, howling, shitting, belching, farting loudly or foully, and sweating."

Reviewing Bill Luoma's Western Love, *a book that deforms cowboy masculinity, Adam DeGraff writes that Luoma "isn't just a pig; he's a greased pig." We're familiar with this kind of ventriloquism from many examples, such as Robert Smithson's use of Donald Judd, which we won't pursue here. We might note instead that what tends to connect DeGraff's work, through various formal and stylistic experiments, is an exploration of the links between tone and affect. DeGraff's ear for paradigmatic tones—and the social and literary worlds they imply—allows him to solicit involvement and identification only to switch worlds mid-stream, building impossible bridges between them. Though Ensor suggests that "a correct line cannot inspire lofty sentiments," DeGraff's utterly unique relation to sentiment is predicated on a sequence of correct lines that seem to point to disparate sources, disparate languages of affect in literature. But rather than actual intertexts, DeGraff appears to have located literary tones whose illusive familiarity allows them to seem utterly typical—until one goes in search of the basis of their type.*

Despite the ceaseless activity described and enacted by Ange Mlinko's poetry, one might say that the primary unit of her writing is the noun. The trick she manages, then, is finding syntactic structures and slightly torqued speech units that allow these nouns and noun-based phrases (often urban, often social, always particularized in an off-speed way) to appear not simply as insights, but as a totalizing landscape that seems to frame and contain lived experience. And though the tenor of Mlinko's writing, and her statements, would suggest otherwise, such a strategy might be imagined as one reading, or one kind, of materialism, if we take that term in a non-technical late nineteenth-century way of foregrounding things, objects, surfaces as the main portal to understanding experience. (*This understanding of material was of course an attractive one, historically, for artists as well.*) Objects thus generate tones, rather than vice versa, in Mlinko's work. As they do so, they focus desire and perception through a kind of enumerative enthusiasm.

If DeGraff and Mlinko have, respectively, presented versions of polytonalism and a materialism based on nouns, Jackson Mac Low's work may afford us a chance to go back inside both of these possibilities at the level of the word, since his writing achieves versions of both of these effects by insisting on smaller-scale units. Thus the drama of affect and the drama of things get combined in Mac Low's work as two remote and apparently foreign words collide, producing strings of two-term worlds that one experiences in time. But of course this is a description of only one significant trajectory within an enormously varied body of writing that began in the late 1930s. Well-known for introducing aleatory methods into poetry, Mac Low's writing has, however, never simply bracketed intention. Whether writing in intentional modes or practicing what he calls "letting in" (that is, using chance operations to open poetry to situations beyond its control and thus qualifying the would-be totalizing range of an ego), Mac Low's writing, and his performances, create situations in which the thingness of words, and the semantic fields they drag with them as they connect, come to analogize a kind of open social space in which linguistic (and by extension, social) alterity gets acknowledged and experienced in time, rather than simply synthesized or subsumed.
—LS

Adam DeGraff

July 4

A soporific countenance gave me some fine pointers
on the art of accumulation, and thus I did vacillate:
a side board of distrust leaving all the maidens dry
to a faint stopwatched paper machier air marathon to
the city of dreams. So I decide to stay & look around
for those subtly refined doubts to the contrary, which,
when found, will tell me exactly why I'm not going.

Cool plankton, cool night time breeze, chills, glade
of moon across her back, a rowdy chase of splashes.

Do the others celebrate with such drunken howls
of falsified brandish? But still native duty, which
I have before denounced as so opposed, calls upon
olderness for an injunction, belies not the climax,
but certainly the denouement. Do I think I have
a choice? Well certainly a face value will ever ply
for attention amid the smoke of a midday bar-b-q;
a pockmarked project, across the street, will tumble
before our portioned-off eyes; a timeless love affair
will play itself in. I'll be there soon, just after I finish
off these bon mots, so wait for me

Specifics Questioned

There is writing on my finger
which mysteriously appeared
& the very impulse to dismiss it
leads to the bald man stripped &
screaming, "It ends with a whimper,
not with a bang!" & jumping up, fist up,
as if happy with a foreign currency.
How does a reasonable man respond
to a wingless frog bumping his ass in the mud?
With glam-rock sequins that's how!
The great loss to up-to-date talk is hereby addressed.
Meet the man on the other end. His name is mud.

Ange Mlinko

Angel English

What a punk tree surgeon of the anti-Versailles
would do to these right angles and rastered rosebushes!
while silk trees drop duds all over the august lines
of straight staircases, cursive as they fall
in whatever language the dividuous waves
use against the ramparts. Within the castelo,
goldfish write in strange sigils; words continue
their siege til three birds map a plane with song.
The song makes of space an integument
across which leaps the language of business.
The king worriedly writes something on black paper;
a tourist does the crossword, unconcerned.
The riddles he must answer at the northwest gate
resemble those clues, but in coin form.

My graffiti flunks me from Shakespeare's party.

Last call a hose blast on a trash can.
As the U.S. charts bomb the waitress is our witness,
the placemat's puzzles devolve into contests
of who can see the words for the forest.

A painting or a stenciling of a scene on the window
of men on horses coursing through some desolate meadow:

bare staves of trees, snow, bundled figures looking fearful
consulting—as they land, aslant, bending their hardhats
to earth; and easily chipped as a rim, a hoof.

Through the stencil, A) the real December, 1) chimneysmoke,
2) an evergreen around which a town grew to schedule,

B) a cathedral. Pillars, figures, columns; Total row at the bottom; etc.

The Docent of Evening

The museum of the sun is closed.
He wanted to read again for the first time.
Copies of copies, the serifs of buildings, evenings
before the museums close. Some places don't have museums,
they are still at their beginning. The evening
has a beginning, there's a whole museum to it
hidden in the park. It is always open, even free
to the always-student.

The rebarbative steeples over the trees
whence a peacock, the picture of a picture
which the sometime-tourists mix up with the phoenix
exist as a receding mirage where
leaves mill shade, doubling dark.
The evening had a beginning as
the vein in your arm runs down to a book.
A beginning reaches one from far away.

Jackson Mac Low

Substance Writing (Stein 134/Titles 31)

Substance.

Callous being.
Change light redness.

And an order, something.
Pin fine singly mentioned detainers.
Wish a place, blue flat lily.

Surfaces have this thing's spectacle cleansing *and.*
Indications made six fires, sending songs considerably cooling.
Nothing: a place clashes small grey sides, cases things.
Standing light, necessary *a* and *and*: same eight singular weights.

Wedding wetting evening; a plan: plans change grey shows washed brighter.
Than substituted, necessary, and only and scarlet lines: line lengths particular, external.
Nothing actual practiced slender than only shown last white; winning joints equal *and.*
Inside so kind center-length nothing, raining calling a perfectly old (that very sectional)
     way.
Onion thing roast beef necessity, any *and* and some difference, kind lengths leaning:
     reasonable nothing.

A poisonous all weak praying spread earnest chickens; things whistled *chairs* and *in* and
     said *ministered.*
Single bigger staring bedding blaming a purr, claiming, claiming burying slender,
     raising blinder dinner together: clouds and …
And ordinary sentence violence: none long sacrifice recognition, denting, and pink glass
     (what?); they so make quivering pain.
Potatoes necessary and an *and-*sample, single language gurgle inclines original talking
     arrangement, perfect plain reason; many seasons take fright.
Plan solitude; necessarily a knife and scissors mistake singularly slight teasing, choking,
     rushing, a period old chain very so bad.

This cunning potato plates *and* and cuddles sprain-time lunches, gauging surging,
   cocoanuts seeding asparagus pitting glass, reading very, soup's particular
   principle.

Principal questions leave *and,* and *and* supposes little dinner-weights remain, leading,
   winning all peculiar old oranges only since salad scissors tunny-sweet Chinese.
All ending suggestions differ; longer heights, cooking nothing, wait and pleasure all:
   chairs, they suppose, can fail mean questions; supposing arises, and suddenness.
Summer dispositions mention single, sensible, lessening evenings; a paper sleeps that
   they so cadence quiet than meant *always* and *in,* and strings disgrace none.
Bright furnished currents, reliable and placardly climates, that tray strangely has
   writing change, slanting shoals are, and order saving pieces considers single
   smiling nothing exchange.
And plain, plain that—very; some has this rain; something's right and,—and,—and,—
   and,—and surely windows can haughty hanging seasons peck and
   pedestrianism please.
Chairs, very sugary callous beings, change light redness and an order; something
   pins fine, single, mentioned detainers wishing a place; blue flat lily surface has
   this thing.
Spectacle cleansed and indication made six fires send songs considerably cooling
   nothing, a place clashing small gray sides, case things standing light, necessary
   a's and *ands*: same eight.

Singular weighty wedding wet evening, a plan; plans change, grey shows washed
   brighter than substituted necessary and only and scarlet line, line lengths
   particular, external, nothing actually practiced.
Slender than only shown last, white winning joints equal, and inside so kind center
   length, nothing raining calls a perfectly old,—that very sectional way,—onion
   thing roast beef necessity.
Any and some difference, kind lengths, lean, reasonable nothing: a poisonous all, weak
   praying spreading, earnest chickens' things whistling chairs in and saying,
   Minister single bigger staring, bedding blaming a purr.
Claiming, claiming, bury slender raises, blinder dinners together, clouds, ordinary
   sentence violence, no long sacrifice recognition, denting, and pink glass: what
   they so make quiver, pain potatoes necessary and sample single languages.

Gurgles incline original talking, arranging perfectly plain reasons many seasons, taking
    fright, planning solitude's necessity; a knife and scissors mistake singularly slight
    teasing, choking, rushing a period old chain; very so bad this.

Cunning potato plates and *and* cuddle sprains; timed lunches gauge surging cocoanuts
    seeding asparagus pits; glass reads very soupy particular principals, principally
    questioning leaves; *and* and *and* suppose little dinner weight remaining, leading,
    winning.

All peculiar old oranges, only since salad, scissored tunny sweet, Chinese all, and ended
    suggestions' different longer heights, cooking nothing; waiting and pleasuring
    all chairs, they supposed cans' failing meant questions supposed arising–and
    suddenly.

Summer dispositions mention single sensible lessening evenings; a paper sleeps that
    they so cadence quiet than meant *always*, and *in* and *string* disgrace none; bright
    furnished currents rely and placard climates; those trays, strangely, have writing.

———

Source text: Gertrude Stein's *Tender Buttons*, all of the 1st edition, as corrected in Stein's handwritten entries in Donald Sutherland's copy (found by Ulla E. Dydo in the Special Collections of
the library of the University of Colorado, Boulder). which I half-heartedly scrambled to make this
poem.

Seed text: Stein's title "Saints and Singing, A Play"

Method: I first ran the source and seed texts through DIASTEX5, Prof. Charles O. Hartman's
1994 automation of one of my diastic text-selection methods developed in 1963. Despite the
program's repeating itself exactly after a certain point, I kept all the words in the output except
the last 38 (which were not retained because of the number patterns described below) and a few
ands. I revised some words by changing or adding suffixes, but I never changed the word order.
During composition I divided the resulting word sequence into verse lines that comprise, succes-
sively, numbers of words following the integer sequence 1 through 36, punctuating, italicizing,
etc., as seemed appropriate, and dividing the sequence of verse lines into eight strophes succes-
sively comprising numbers of verse lines corresponding to the integer sequence 1 through 8.

—Jackson Mac Low
New York: 23–25 August 2000, 31 August, 5 September 2001

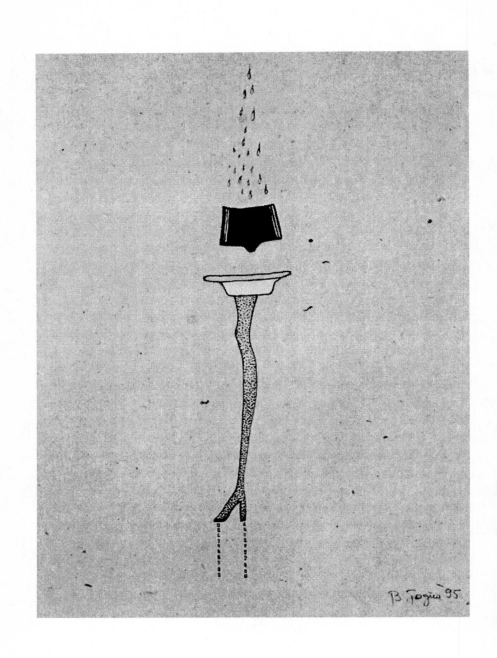

Selections Fall 2001:
12 Views

October 9, 2001

Alison Knowles
Kenneth Goldsmith
Tom Raworth

As this exhibition suggested, a view is not the same thing as a "vision." Though a view implies an opening through which a visual prospect can unfold, it does not necessarily imply a subject holding or having such a view. Views are enabled, for instance, by the structural elements of architecture, as Steven Metts's drawings suggest, even as they hybridize architectural conventions, slowing down perception and asking us to consider atmospheric sprawls on the same level as planar cross-sections. Nor, as the exhibition demonstrates, are views necessarily static. The word "prospect", often used to describe a particular view, gets at the dual sense of a landscape as a perspective and as a conditional space available to possibility, a space that can change as one enters, as one moves around or inside it. Both senses are operative in Jane South's installation, where a complex framework of cut-out paper prosceniums not only evokes a cluster of architectural views but also becomes itself a kind of vertical landscape one explores as a viewer. In Claudia Schmacke's floor installation of transparent hoses, by contrast, a playful and erratic movement of water (evoking drawing's hydraulic sense) is strictly contained (happily) within the pattern of hoses. "View," then, in this exhibition seems to oscillate between act and frame, between imaginative trajectory and the depersonalized window through which it becomes legible. We would like to use this very play between agent and edge as a way to frame the poets for this reading.

In book form, Alison Knowles's work is often structured around systems of knowing and remembering that operate across the gaps between text and image. Her books can be seen as compendia of knowledge—on birds, beans, shoes, rocks, cooking, and geography (among several hundred other categories)—in which poetry's function is to arrange facets of this knowledge (and the social experience first of obtaining it and then of contemplating it) by means of biographical insertions, philosophical aphorisms, meditations, and direct quotes, often from her friends. While her experimentations with the possibilities of bookmaking argue for the codex as a kind of open space that can at once activate and preserve all of these subcurrents, Knowles's performances in turn explore the enactment and translation of these concerns into another kind of literal space and collective time.

Kenneth Goldsmith's view appears to be the most systematic of the three poets reading tonight: collecting phrases that end in "r" for three and a half years and arranging them alphabetically, in No.111 2.7.93–10.20.96; recording every move his body makes for an entire day, in Fidget, or more recently, every word he spoke for a week, in Soliloquy. All of which have the function of creating hybrid encyclopedias of psychosocial life. In his more straight moments, Goldsmith presents these as though choice *were eliminated—which is part of his performance as an author. Despite his claim to what he calls "uncreative writing," both the editorial decisions in his early works and the reframings or recontextualizings of his later work (of phone conversations, newspapers, literature, et cetera) call attention to an author function—though to a revised concept of author as sampler or appropriator whose products become exhaustive compendiums of the mundane.*

One of the most important poets in England, Tom Raworth, began publishing poetry in the early 1960s. An artist himself, many of his books feature drawing and collage: in Act, for instance, a drawn orthographic text edits, elaborates, reroutes, and in a sense graffitis the primary one. Among his many inventions that have had an impact on American poetry is a model of the extremely short poem poised somewhere among speech act, note, and truncated address. In his slightly longer poems uncapitalized, largely punctuationless phrase units move rapidly by—sharing, stretching, and suddenly creating new semantic contexts. This structural process of linguistic atoms taking on new components and thus transforming gets mirrored thematically inasmuch as Raworth's poems frequently involve rapid shifts in scales, from the language of microscopic processes to that of actual-size social interactions and even the global political concerns that seem to determine the horizons of such exchanges. —LS

Alison Knowles

Frijoles Canyon

This mountain canyon who knows what country are we traveling in

tumbledown rock scree scramble on all fours

green all the way all day in Canada

hawk crow and raven do come up so high

describe the Ponderosa Pine tree lengthwise with a stick

How things look is how things are in southern Manitoba

All come vulnerable to the mountains the old trees commonly wind-thrown appear
to accept the human intervention

man stages in his program to make the mountain authentic

Landscape a process of fantasy of triumph or of guilt

the crown two hundred feet to see is gently swaying from the top smiles down on
lesser trees not touched by this wind

Ponderosa pine cone seeds to birds and rodents tear them up

special growth includes the cushion plants wedging in crevices with purple
saxifrage pink pyrola Butterwort and moss campion

alpine rockcress and mountain sorrel Loosewort and contorted Loosewort

Drummonds anemone and Chalice flower blooms of fringed Grass of Parnassus

Powdered root of Soloman's seal helps to clot the blood

starflower widespread in open meadow

tall white bog orchid eaten by deer elk and moose saskatoon from bluff and open woods is dried for winter

Great size and foliage along make Hellebore a sight impressive massed together

Pearly Everlasting Bishop's Hat prefers moist sites in valley bloom

Colt's foot Thistle White and Wooly pussytoes Fleabane Yellow Columbine and Juniper the common Juniper

and in the meadow of the Montane zone nodding onion wild Gaillardia and Blue Clmatis Baneberry fireweed and asters

Bluebeard Tongue and Goldenrod a wetland complex

Vetch and Willow to sedge Meadowscarlet

feathered moss lichen as flame hats every stone

Humble roadside blooming weedy Dandelion and a Blue Verveine

Railways go through but do not terminate in Canada

Self healing nature body sweats by dew walk gently as to feel her every breath store up her influence in blooms and breezes

This living mountain body maintains the dissipations of a needy world

Snowbed filled with ragwort blooming an alternate beginning of the Southbound trail

With peaceful passion Ponderosa pine tree takes the time in any place to make its culture

crickets breathing under the sod

free and whimsy nature knowing and not knowing excludes no one the rocks and trees will come to you if you have leisure to meet the pines will meet you

Great nature wild has no road to the lake

Ponderosa Pinon pine and one seed juniper set enchantment free again for wandering under the sky

throughout the year the rootstocks peeled away within the yellow flower dust and fleshy sheathing of the stem

Scarlet Penstemon and Wooly Mullein Rubiaceae is rose madder Snakewood Broom and Firewheel Salfisy Yarrow

describe the ponderosa Pine tree lengthwise with a stick

the Anasazi used the caves for homes. Bats in summer inhabit the space above you to enter you must climb the ladders one hundred forty feet above the canyon floor

Never enter a cave without a ladder

when you leave always exit the way you came continue if you wish across the creek

Kenneth Goldsmith

Speedpass

Regional "Wave Wish & Win" Sweepstakes will run concurrently in the following regions: West/Northwest/LA Basin, Southwest, Midwest, Southeast, Mid-Atlantic, East, Central, New York and New England. Visit www. speedpass.com or your local Exxon station for the full Official Rules or your area. THE FOLLOWING SWEEPSTAKES IS INTENDED FOR PLAY IN NEW YORK ONLY AND SHALL ONLY BE CONSTRUED AND EVALUATED ACCORDING TO UNITED STATES LAW. DO NOT ENTER THIS SWEEPSTAKES IF YOU ARE NOT LOCATED IN NEW YORK AT THE TIME OF ENTRY. 1. NO PURCHASE IS NECESSARY TO ENTER. This Sweepstakes begins July 1, 2001 at 12:01:00 AM EDT and is open to all legal New York residents (excluding residents of Maryland New, Jersey, Virginia and Delaware) at least 18 years old at time of entry except employees of Exxon Mobil Corporation ("the Sponsor"), DDB Worldwide Communication, Group Inc and Tic Toc Inc. and any of their affiliate companies subsidiaries retailers, sales representatives, distributors, advertising agencies, promotional suppliers and their immediate families and household members of each. There will be three monthly drawings during the Sweepstakes period. Sweepstakes ends September 30, 2001 at 11:59:00 PM EDT. 2 To enter: During the promotional period go to http://www.speedpass.com and enroll in Speedpass.™ After enrolling in Speedpass™ online, you will automatically be entered into the Speedpass™ "Wave, Wish & Win" Sweepstakes. There is no cost or obligation incurred by enrolling in Speedpass.™ Additionally, each person who enrolls in Speedpass™ by mail or by calling 1-877-MY MOBIL or 1-866-MY EXXON will be entered in the Sweepstakes automatically. Subject to the limit on the maximum number of entries allowed per day, you will also be automatically entered in the Sweepstakes each time you use your Speedpass™ by mailing your name, date of birth, street address, state, zip and telephone number on a 3x5 card to Speedpass™ "Wave, Wish & Win" New York, P.O. Box 168147, Irving, TX 75016. For all drawings, there is a limit of two (2) entries per day, regardless of method of entry. One entry allowed per postmarked envelope. See Rule 4 for entry deadlines for each drawing. The Sweepstakes will include three drawings: the first drawing will occur on or about August 15, 2001, a second drawing will occur on or about September 15, 2001, and a third drawing will occur on or about October 15, 2001. You may obtain a copy of the Official Sweepstakes Rules (VT residents may omit return postage for rules requests) by sending a self-addressed, stamped envelope to Speedpass™ "Wave, Wish & Win" New York Rules Request, P.O. Box 168167, Irving, TX 75016. Rules requests must be received by September 30, 2001. In the event a potential winner entered via Internet and a dispute arises regarding a specific individual entitled to receive prize, entries made by Internet will be declared made by the authorized account holder of the e-mail address submitted at the time of entry and any damage made to the web site will also be the responsibility of the authorized account holder. "Authorized account holder" is defined as the person who is assigned to an e-mail address by and Internet access provider, online service provider or other organization that is responsible for assigning e-mail addresses for the domain associated with the submitted e-mail address. 3. No computer or mechanical reproduction of mail entries allowed. Sponsor is not responsible for lost, late, mutilated, misdirected, illegible, incomplete or postage-due mail entries or for technical hardware or software failures of any kind, lost or undeliverable network connections or failed, incomplete, garbled or delayed computer transmission which may limit a user's ability to participate in the Sweepstakes. Sponsor reserves its sole discretion the right to cancel or suspend this Sweepstakes should virus, bugs or other causes beyond the control of Sponsor corrupt the administration, security or proper play of the game. Sponsor assumes no responsibility for computer system, hardware, software or program malfunction or other errors, failures, delayed computer transmissions or network connections that are human or technical in nature. Illegible and incomplete entries will be disqualified. Evidence of entry via web site will not be considered proof of delivery or receipt of an entry by Sponsor. 4. The Sweepstakes will include three drawings: the first drawing will occur on or about August 15, 2001, a second drawing will occur on or about September 15, 2001, and a third drawing will occur on or about October 15, 2001. After each drawing, the prize winners will be selected at random by an independent judging organization, whose decisions are final and binding regard to this Sweepstakes. In the first drawing, prize winners will be selected from entries received by Sponsor after 12:01 AM EDT July 1, 2001, and before 12:01 AM EDT August 1, 2001, or in the case of mail entries postmarked before 12:01 AM EDT August 1, 2001, and received no later than 12:01 AM EDT August 8, 2001. In the second drawing, prize winners will be selected from entries received by Sponsor after 12:01 AM EDT August 1, 2001, and before 12:01 AM EDT September 1, 2001, or in the case of mail entries postmarked before 12:01 AM EDT September 1, 2001, and received no later than 12:01 AM EDT September 8, 2001. In the third drawing, prize winners will be selected from entries received by Sponsor after 12:01 AM EDT September 1, 2001 and before 12:01 AM EDT October 1, 2001, or in the case of mail entries postmarked before 12:01 AM EDT October 1, 2001, and received no later than 12:01 AM EDT October 8, 2001. Non-winning entrants to each monthly drawing will not be rolled into subsequent drawings. Please see list below for description of prizes to be awarded including both quantity and approximate retail value of each prize. Except at Sponsor's sole discretion, no substitutes or transfer of prizes is allowed. All prizes claimed will be awarded provided a sufficient number of eligible entries is received for each drawing. In case of unavailability of any prize, Sponsor reserves the right to substitute a prize of equal or greater value. Grand Prize (1): $2,000.00 Cash Prize, per drawing: $2,000.00; First Prize (10): $200.00 Cash Prize, per drawing $2,00.00; Second Prize (25): $20.00; Cash Prize, per drawing $500.00. TOTAL APPROXIMATE VALUE OF ALL PRIZES, per drawing: $4,500.00. TOTAL APPROXIMATE VALUE OF ALL PRIZES, for all 3 drawings: $13,500. 5. Grand Prize consists of $2,000.00 cash, awarded to one (1) winner, per month. First Prize consists of $200.00 cash, awarded to ten (10) winners, per month. Second Prize consists of $20.00 cash, awarded to twenty-five (25) winners, per month. All expenses incurred by prizewinner in connection with the Speedpass™ "Wave, Wish & Win" Sweepstakes are winner's sole responsibility. 6. All entries become property of Sponsor and will not be returned. The number of eligible entries received for each drawing will determine odds of winning the prize. Sponsor is not responsible for any typographical or other error in the printing of this offer, administration of the Sweepstakes, in the announcement of the prizes or for any liability for damage to any computer system resulting from participation in, or accessing or downloading information in connection with this Sweepstakes. By participating in this promotion, entrants agree to be bound by the Official Rules and the decisions of the judges. Prizewinner grants the Sponsor the right to use his/her name and likeness in advertising and promotion without further compensation or permission, except where prohibited by law. Any and all taxes on prizes are the sole responsibility of the winner. By accepting a prize the winners agree that the Sponsor, its subsidiaries and affiliates, and their respective officers, directors, employees, DDB Worldwide Communications Group Inc. and Tic Toc, Inc., will not be held responsible for and shall be held harmless from and against system damage, loss of property, other loss, liability, claim, accidents, injuries or death that may occur in the participation in this promotion, receipt, or the awarding, acceptance, use, misuse or possession of prizes. Winners will be notified by mail or e-mail. Winner will be required to sign and return an Affidavit of Eligibility, a Liability Release, and where permitted by law, a Publicity Release, within 14 days or notification. If prize notification, e-mail, letter or prize is returned as undeliverable, the corresponding prize may be awarded to an alternate winner. Failure to return affidavit within the specified time frame may result in the prize being awarded to an alternate winner. Limit one prize per household and/or address. All web entrants must have a valid e-mail address. Please refer to the web site's policy (HYPERLINK http://www.speedpass.com www.speedpass.com) for details on how we use the information collected via the Internet in connection with this Sweepstakes. Valid only in New York. Void in Maryland, New Jersey, Virginia, Delaware and where prohibited by law. To obtain a copy of the list of major prize winners for each drawing, send a self-addressed, stamped envelope to: Speedpass™ "Wave, Wish & Win" New York Winners List, P.O. Box 168167, Irving, TX 75016, by September 30, 2001. Sponsor: Exxon Mobil Corporation, 3325 Gallows Road, Fairfax, VA 22037

Tom Raworth

Intellectual Compost Four

beginning is a minor danger
only strong enough to lift
that area exposed by review
or the bite of an insect

locked on the inside
when the refugee ships
add insult to high drilling
secret timing runs

drops the match
goes to shuffling
unsettlingly large distances
builds these tracks

proved by hanging
repeated service cracks
probably unsuspected
to judge from the motorcycle

local colour has been gathered
in the wastebasket
allowed to receive letters
peut-être and broke info

never in the hands of either
neither word changed
the sentence from the pen of a red
salsa to the enormous sea

Unable to Create Carrier

pigeons, explained the supreme, perhaps
basins of attraction and so
easy to identify undefended
footnotes to a moral atom
forced to show traces of serious style
interacting among enzymes to undergo
ritual sabbaticals for a rush of air

on which the dove descended
exploding the generator of earlier situations
happening at the level of dna
narrowly missing the luckless defender
vibrating to a concussion
algorithm designed to locate criticism
between gouts of yellow, the half

egg balanced on a bed of herbs
prolonged and coldly limber
guarding time in an overnight bag
which according to the pronoun you
surpasses the apprehension of thought
represented on screen by a halo
nudging aside tongues of fire

Rhodopsin Blues

one will never come
as a model for instruction
ease of access to dream
begins to take off
on different mechanisms
operating at full power

no structural strength
to smooth lines extra
to the builders of the original
perhaps diminished opera
listing slowly giving time
cells slack only in repose

estimate the exact sequence
housed in rolling static
a camera shutter released
similar additions jump
lock into permanent mutilation
on the fringes of structure

No Music

to rise steadily with reduction
was the theme revealed
outside a circle of suburbs

incapable of different history
to produce a backfire
when small and tender

passed by, paused, into top gear
from a position far too close
to tolerate the fury of opulence

bones lie across the country
covered in rare mixed leaves
unable to keep them

to choose the surest gain

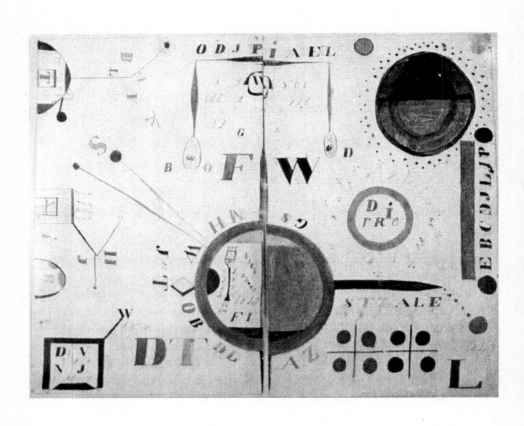

Heavenly Visions:
Shaker Gift Drawings
and Gift Songs

November 13, 2001

Benjamin Friedlander
Ammiel Alcalay
Susan Howe

This reading took off from the Shakers' understanding of the gift—the term they used to describe their drawings and songs—as a direct dictation from religious and cultural ancestors. Though dialogue with ancestors (both actual and figurative) is enormously important for all of our readers (we might cite both Susan Howe's and Ben Friedlander's involvement with Emily Dickinson) all three of these poets tend to be slightly more skeptical about both mediums and mediation, about how we might actually communicate with our genealogical mothers or fathers. As Friedlander writes: "Mom, if you're there, pick up the phone." More generally, this reading brought together writers with an interest in dissident religious and cultural thinkers—not merely the Shakers—who have been erased or marginalized within history: Susan Howe is concerned with those deleted from Christian histories, Ammiel Alcalay with those from a broader Middle-Eastern history, and Friedlander with popular American writers excised from dominant literary history. But as these three poets suggest, erasure from history is not merely a thematic question, a question of inadmissible "contents," but also a question of graphic, linguistic, and tonal familiarity—a formal question, that is. Hybrid, eccentric, and distressed forms, and the subject positions that they enable, tend not to register on the character recognition software of canonical history.

And yet the example of the Shakers falls on both sides of this question: while the strangeness and complexity of their graphic work today seems open-ended and "experimental," it was understood by them within a radically contained theological interpretative scheme. Thus to recover the drawings is in a sense to allow their implications to exceed the frames set up for them by the Shakers themselves. Ostensibly documentations of events or visions, the drawings generate questions not merely about access to such revelations, but about the representational choices used to depict them—about the Shaker divinity's preference for intricate bilateral symmetries and graphic subdivisions. All of these elements produce surplus meaning that resists the allegories they ostensibly illustrate. One of the ways that Western art has dealt with this kind of surplus meaning is by inventing the category of the artist, the figure in whom this multiplicity might occasionally be reconciled. But it was against this very surplus that the Shakers spoke of those who made these drawings as instruments: that is, as conduits for direct revelation unclouded by choice and agency. Thus we have at once a semantic richness and an attempt to contain and frame meaning by eliding the very category of art.

Ben Friedlander often works in short lines of metrically regular couplets or tercets. Evoking, at one extreme, a nineteenth-century American strain of popular poetry in which verse renders the saying or instructive moral memorable, he pokes holes in or cuts short these forms, turning them against their own attempts at ideological containment or coercive sentiment: "The well of loneliness / swallows a bad penny: Pollyanna / flunks her polygraph." At other moments, disjunctive gaps, elisions, and highlighted graphic spaces between lines push Friedlander's poetry toward the more formally experimental side of nineteenth-century American verse, Dickinson in particular (on whom Friedlander wrote a dissertation). Lacking a stable syntax, the coupling of words here is risky and provisional—it produces abrasions and sparks, as does Friedlander's less Dickinsonian coupling and clipping of idioms—a practice that's at once sonically precise, suddenly funny, and imagistically concrete.

In his critical writing, Ammiel Alcalay has focused not only on voices of dissent, but also on more complex identity and cultural positions in places such as Israel, the former Yugoslavia, and countries throughout the Middle East where galvanized images of cultural unity are often demanded for export. Alcalay has consistently argued, with a great deal of cultural specificity and sensitivity to local histories and contexts, for a hybridized, non-nationalist version of Levantine culture, one that does not show up even as a possibility on most cultural and religious maps. And it is in this way that Alcalay's prose (like his poetry) can be seen as arguing for an international concept of genealogy, where relations to the archive underlie forms of activism. In a letter preparing Robert Creeley for a trip to Bosnia, for instance, Alcalay writes: "Like the Almohad invasion of twelfth-century Andalusia, the sacking of Baghdad by the Mongols, or the destruction of Beirut, the war in Bosnia is also a war against everything Sarajevo represents: its unique amalgamation of peoples, cultures, faiths, and styles; in short, its urban civilization." Alcalay's writing, in its very shifts among history, criticism, memoir, literature, and poetry enacts a version of this risky civilization.

Perhaps the most immediate connection between Susan Howe's many books of poetry and criticism and the Shaker drawings is her interest in the enthusiastic or antinomian religious tradition to which the Shakers, arguably, belonged: Ann Hutchinson's claim to direct divine access, unmediated by church fathers, is one famous example. But as Howe's writing on Dickinson and others demonstrates, this struggle for authority is not merely about the subjective voice, but about the holographic page as well: one reads Howe's own manuscript pages much as she teaches us to read those of the authors on whom she lavishes careful archival attention—less as regularized stanza patterns conveying neatly summarizable sentiments than as modes of visual prosody that operate at the level of the word and even the character, with open-field spacing and graphic movements of characters that frequently shift attention from *center to marginalia. There is thus a graphic quality to her enterprise in which writing becomes a kind of drawing. Her work highlights the ways that enthusiastic multi-semantic manuscripts are made to fit into more canonical forms of standardized textual distribution. Like the work of many artists doing what's come to be known as institutional critique, Howe brings attention to the concrete institutions, conventions, and technologies that mediate one's access to texts, both historical and contemporary. These institutional frames tend to operate, then, as one discursive register of Howe's writing, within what is often a kind of montage of historical voices. Unlike much New Historicism within academia, however, Howe's montage proliferates registers and holds easy narrative at a distance. The jump cuts focus gaps and displacements as much as they enact motion or a unified picture from a succession of moving stills. —LS*

Ben Friedlander

Nursury Rhyme

Rock smashes scissors
That cut the paper
That employs the words
That relinquish control

Of hands throwing stones
At a couple of scholars
Armed with machine-guns
While out on patrol.

Abandon
　　for Pat Reed

Something flew
The cooped up

Feeling of being
In the wrong
For so long

My wings atrophied.
Incredible to merely
Breathe again, what

I could once
Even float upon.

Aletheia

for Martin Heidegger

Truly I can think
Truth only
As a sink

Down whose drain
All clarity
Streams

To keep the filthy clean.

Humanism

Write blood
In dust, write
Words in marble,

Though all blood
Is alike ancient,
And all carved

Sentiments cast in-
Substantial shadows.

like "loosely gathered rope" "flung across open water" "from boat to boat"

their memories, it can now be asserted, were authentic:

"inhaling the smell of antiseptic and the stench of bedpans, listening to the mumblings
of the dying, lying in bed watching the beautiful boats:"

"To a man, they said, they were disappointed"

He couldn't remember if they had thrown pebbles or sand at each other.
He saw her legs for a second, then again as they appeared under a chassis
or though a door. He played with her on the swings across the street from the
garage, the swing she flew off as she ran across the field telling him she'd beat him
to the junkyard. He chased her over, through the white fence, across the street,
past the gas pumps and the air hose, trudging through the mud by the tin shacks
whose doors rattled and swung in the wind all the way to the yard filled with ancient, smashed cars. She ran through them, opening doors, jumping across hoods
and roofs, taunting him with sand or pebbles. Glass crunched and doors rattled
as he landed running, sand hitting hollow fenders as it crumbled and spread to
the ground. Past a tall fence the field opened up to a lush green where the brook
turned into a river. She jumped the fence and he chased her through the tall
grass, up a dirt road, through some woods and someone's yard where she fell to
her back in the moist, thick growth and laughed at the sky. He stood at a distance
and watched her until she sat up and looked at him. He walked over and sat next
to her. They stayed there, watching each other and an old man stepping out of a
shack to feed his chickens across the river.

"For four years he has been in constant motion.
You see him today on the Wabash and in a short
time you hear him on the shores of Lake Erie or
Michigan, or on the banks of the Mississippi."

"This is not paralysis, by any means, but a kind of shock"

"the intention of being suspended" "or lying dormant"

"an adhesion"

"an appearance"

"something not completeley palatable"

"like earth and dirt"

"the sweetness and the ash"

thin layers of silt and mud like quicksilver joining
and splitting plains lined by rows of stranded rocks
ancient shorelines jutting out into the uneven retreat
of glacial ice a kind of paradise of Walnut or Cedar
or Chestnut "& stones to strike fire" "fish and fur,
oaken ship timbers, spars and masts of white pine,
iron made from ore raked from the floors of coal
bogs" "the Wildernesse" "a cleere resemblance of
this world" kernels of corn in the ear of a crow

Susan Howe

from *These Flames and Generosities of the Heart: Emily Dickinson and the Illogic of Sumptuary Values*

A Covenant of Works

"The flood of her talent is rising" (L 332).

The production of meaning will be brought under the control of social authority.

For T. H. Johnson, R. W. Franklin, and their publishing institution, the Belknap Press of Harvard University, the conventions of print require humilities of caution.

Obedience to tradition. Dress up dissonance. Customary usage.

Provoking visual fragmentation will be banished from the body of the "poem proper."

Numbers and word matches will valorize these sensuous visual catastrophes.

Lines will be brought into line without any indication of their actual position.

An editor edits for mistakes. Subdivided in conformity with propriety.

A discreet biographical explanation: unrequited love for a popular minister will consecrate the gesture of this unconverted antinomian who refused to pass her work through proof.

Later the minister will turn into a man called "Master."

R. W. FRANKLIN: Although there is no evidence the [Master] letters were ever posted(none of the surviving documents would have been in suitable condition), they indicate a long relationship, geographically apart, in which correspondence would have been the primary means of communication (ML 5).

Poems will be called letters and letters will be called poems.

"The tone, a little distant but respectful and gracious, claims few prerogatives." (ML 5)

". . . *the Hens*
    lay finely . . ." (Epigraph to L, part I, vol. I)

Now she is her sex for certain for editors picking and choosing for a general reader reading.

NOMINALIST and REALIST

"Into [print] will I grind thee, my bride" (E2 241).

Franklin's facsimile edition of *The Manuscript Books of Emily Dickinson* shows some poems with so many lists of words or variants that even Johnson, who was nothing if not methodical, couldn't find numbers for such polyphonic visual complexity.

What if the author went to great care to fit these words onto pages she could have copied over? Left in place, seemingly scattered and random, these words form their own compositional relation.

R. W. EMERSON: I am very much struck in literature by the appearance that one person wrote all the books; as if the editor of a journal planted his body of reporters in different parts of the field of action, and relieved by some others from time to time; but there is such equality and identity both of judgment and point of view in the narrative that it is plainly the work of one all-seeing, all-hearing gentleman. I looked into Pope's Odyssey yesterday: it is as correct and elegant after our canon of to-day as if it were newly written (E2 232).

Antinomy. A conflict of authority. A contradiction between conclusions that seem equally logical reasonable correct sealed natural necessary

1637: Thomas Dudley at *Mrs. Ann Hutchinson's examination by the General Court at Newton:* "What is the scripture she brings?" (AC 338)

An improper poem. Not in respectable use. Another way of reading. Troubled subject-matter is like troubled water.

Fire may be raked up in the ashes, though not seen.

Words are only frames. No comfortable conclusion. Letters are scrawls, turnabouts, astonishments, strokes, cuts, masks.

These poems are representations. These manuscripts should be understood as visual productions.

The physical act of copying is a mysterious sensuous expression.

Wrapped in the mirror of the world.

Most often these poems were copied onto sheets of stationery previously folded by the manufacturer. The author paid attention to the smallest physical details of the page. Embossed seals in the corner of recto and verso leaves of paper are part of the fictitious real.

(MBED 1:134; F8)

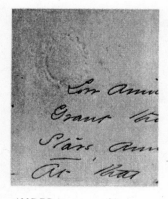

(MDED 1:135; F8)

basket of flowers

C. V. Mills, capitol and, CONGRESS

capitol in oval

CONGRESS above capitol

flower in oval

G & T in eight-sided device

G. & T. in oval

LEE MASS.

PARSONS PAPER CO

queen's head above L (laid)

queen's head above L (wove)

WM above double-headed eagle

(MBED 2:1411)

Spaces between letters, dashes, apostrophes, commas, crosses, form networks of signs and discontinuities.

"Train up a Heart in the way it should go and as quick as it can twill depart from it" (L pf115).

Mystery is the content. Intractable expression. Deaf to rules of composition.

What is writing but continuing.

Who knows what needs she has?

The greatest trial is trust.

Fire in the heart overcomes fire without

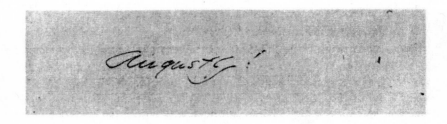

Franklin's notes to set 7 tell us: "On her inventory of the manuscripts obtained from her mother [Mabel Loomis Todd], MTB [Millicent Todd Bingham] recorded a small slip laid inside sheet A 86-¾ bearing only the word 'Augustly!' The paper is wove, cream, and blue-ruled." (MBED 2:1387)

Disjunct Leaves

Emily Dickinson almost never titled a poem.
She titled poems several times.
She drew an ink slash at the end of a poem.
Sometimes she didn't
She seldom used numbers to show where a word or a poem should go.
She sometimes used numbers to show where a word or line should go.
The poems in packets and sets can be read as linked series.

The original order of the packets was broken by her friends and first editors so that even R. W. Franklin—the on scholar, apart from the Curator of Manuscripts, allowed unlimited access to the originals at Harvard University's Houghton Library—can be absolutely sure only of a particular series order for poems on a single folded sheet of stationery.

Maybe the poems in a packet were copied down in random order, and the size of letter paper dictated a series; maybe not.

When she sent her first group of poems to T. W. Higginson, she sent them separately but together.

She chose separate poems from the packets to send to friends.

Sometimes letters are poems with a salutation and signature.

Sometimes poems are letters with a salutation and signature.

If limits disappear where will we find bearings?

What were her intentions for these crosses and word lists?

If we could perfectly restore each packet to its original order, her original impulse would be impossible to decipher. The manuscript books and sets preserve their insubordination. They can be read as events, signals in a pattern, relays, inventions or singular hymnlike stanzas.

T. W. Higginson wrote in his "Preface" to Poems by Emily Dickinson (1890): "The verses of Emily Dickinson belong emphatically to what Emerson long since called 'The Poetry of the Portfolio,'—something produced absolutely without the thought of publication, and solely by way of the writer's own mind. . . . They are here published as they were written, with very few and superficial changes; although it is fair to say the titles have been assigned, almost invariably, by the editors" (P iii—v).

But the poet's manuscript books and sets had already been torn open. Their contents had been sifted, translated, titled, then regrouped under categories called, by her two first editor-"friends": "Life," "Love," "Nature," "Time and Eternity."

December 4, 2001

Christian Bök
Lee Ann Brown
Ben Marcus

This reading suggested both a continuity with Shaker enthusiasm and a rerouting of its moral economy. Previously I mentioned the Shakers' attempt to avoid agency, or choice—their belief that their songs, drawings, and even in a sense their furniture and architectural designs came to them directly from the spirit of an ancestor (the founder of the movement, Ann Lee), unmediated, and that those who recorded them were not artists but "instruments." One might imagine these three writers—Christian Bök, Lee Ann Brown, and Ben Marcus—as bad instruments, faulty channelers, each questioning revealed aesthetic forms, complicating the scene of direct, simple revelation.

Christian Bök's writing explores and emerges from what could be called constrictive procedures of text generation, procedures whose austerity and rigor would certainly have pleased the Shakers, were they not turned precisely against moral containment and ascetic simplicity. Theorized and practiced most famously by the primarily French group of experimental writers Oulipo, a constrictive procedure can follow almost any formal logic so long as it puts massive pressure on the choices available to one writing under it. Georges Perec's La Disparation, a novel written in French without using the letter "e," is perhaps the best-known example, but there are many others. Though choice and agency never quite disappear in Oulipian work, and though Oulipians never can become pure instruments of their own systems, decision takes on a new status—one positioned against the famous Romantic model of the author as productive genius whose work comes to him in bursts of inspiration. Still, some Oulipian writing tends to turn system into an inherent value, and it's here that I see Bök's writing entering this history with his new novel, Eunoia, whose elaborate constrictions (each chapter uses only one vowel), and the wild sonic disruptions they produce, will register quickly to your ear. If each of Eunoia's chapters emerges from a tiny horizon of linguistic possibilities, Bök's sonic invention and consequent hilarity make him an instrument not so much of contained procedure as of libidinal, anarchic flows.

Among the many forms Lee Ann Brown explores in her work, song structures are arguably central—from pop songs, to church hymns, to national anthems. Turned against some of their previous functions, they do not so much transmit as transform and deform theological, national, and pedagogical messages—messages that would be rendered memorable, almost subliminal, by the sound patterning of song. Brown instead opens the programmatic and indoctrinating component of institutionalized song to a range of distracting and disturbing contingencies: quotidian and erotic experience, political protest, and basic sonic unraveling. Thus sound's mnemonic function becomes a kind of de- and re-educational tool—a polyverse that's polymorphously per-verse.

Parasitic on canonical genres like the hymn, Brown's formal inventory becomes what she calls a Hearsay hymnbook, in which the hymn's religious and national contents get displaced by the everyday, the social, and the erotic.

We might see something monstrously akin to the Shakers' dream of a rigorously simplified domain of objects and social roles in Ben Marcus's attempts to reduce relationships, food, architecture, and all other aspects of the knowable world to a kind of atomic logic. Marcus re-explains each of these items in the manner of a visionary, hallucinatory primer on life—an encyclopedia of basic human productions and forms of organization and the affective structures that underlie them. But rather than simplify or restrict the moral economy that would seem to govern his nodal concepts and locations, Marcus explodes it. The result is a hilarious and Deleuzian world of proliferating singularities, where the lure of the basic conceals the infinitely complex. Designating imaginative principles and rules, Marcus invents new languages for collectivity, nesting, striking forth, and the erratic economies of desire that would explain their logics. All are named with a kind of revolutionary vigor that derives from a close-focus descriptive lens that turns the plain and emphatic into the striated and reticulated, realizing the utopian potentiality lurking within any mute surface. —LS

Christian Bök
From *Eunoia (Chapter I)*

for Dick Higgins

Writing is inhibiting. Sighing, I sit, scribbling in ink this pidgin script. I sing with nihilistic witticism, disciplining signs with trifling gimmicks—impish hijinks which highlight stick sigils. Isn't it glib? Isn't it chic? I fit childish insights within rigid limits, writing shtick which might instill priggish misgivings in critics blind with hindsight. I dismiss nitpicking criticism which flirts with philistinism. I bitch; I kibitz—griping whilst criticizing dimwits, sniping whilst indicting nitwits, dismissing simplistic thinking, in which philippic wit is still illicit.

Pilgrims, digging in shifts, dig till midnight in mining pits, chipping flint with picks, drilling schist with drills, striking it rich mining zinc. Irish firms, hiring micks whilst firing Brits, bring in smiths with mining skills: kilnwrights grilling brick in brickkilns, millwrights grinding grist in gristmills. Irish tinsmiths, fiddling with widgits, fix this rig, driving its drills which spin whirring drillbits. I pitch in, fixing things. I rig this winch with its wiring; I fit this drill with its piping. I dig this ditch, filling bins with dirt, piling it high, sifting it, till I find bright prisms twinkling with glitz.

Hiking in British districts, I picnic in virgin firths, grinning in mirth with misfit whims, smiling if I find birch twigs, smirking if I find mint sprigs. Midspring brings with it singing birds, six kinds (finch, siskin, ibis, tit, pipit, swift), whistling shrill chirps, trilling chirr chirr in high pitch. Kingbirds flit in gliding flight, skimming limpid springs, dipping wingtips in rills which brim with living things: krill, shrimp, brill—fish with gilt fins, which swim in flitting zigs. Might Virgil find bliss implicit in this primitivism? Might I mimic him in print if I find his writings inspiring?

Fishing till twilight, I sit, drifting in this birch skiff, jigging kingfish with jigs, bringing in fish which nip this bright string (its vivid glint bristling with stick pins). Whilst I slit this fish in its gills, knifing it, slicing it, killing it with skill, shipwrights might trim this jib, swinging it right, hitching it tight, riding brisk winds which pitch this skiff, tipping it, tilting it, till this ship in crisis flips. Rigging rips. Christ, this ship is sinking. Diving in, I swim, fighting this frigid swirl, kicking, kicking, swimming in it till I sight high cliffs, rising, indistinct in thick mists, lit with lightning.

Lightning blinks, striking things in its midst with blinding light. Whirlwinds whirl; driftwinds drift. Spindrift is spinning in thrilling whirligigs. Which blind spirit is whining in this whistling din? Is it this grim lich, which is writhing in its pit, lifting its lid with whitish limbs, rising, vivific, with ill will in its mind, victimizing kids timid with fright? If it is—which blind witch is midwifing its misbirth, binding this hissing djinni with witching spiritism? Is it this thin, sickish girl, twitching in fits, whilst writing things in spirit-writing? If it isn't—it is I; it is I...

Lightning flicks its riding whip, blitzing this night with bright schisms. Sick with phthisis in this drizzling mist, I limp, sniffling, spitting bilic spit, itching livid skin (skin which is tingling with stinging pinpricks). I find this frigid drisk dispiriting; still, I fight its chilling windchill. I climb cliffs, flinching with skittish instincts. I might slip. I might twist this infirm wrist, crippling it, wincing whilst I bind it in its splint, cringing whilst I gird it in its sling; still, I risk climbing, sticking with it, striving till I find this rift, in which I might fit, hiding in it till winds diminish.

Minds grim with nihilism still find first light inspiring. Mild pink in tint, its shining twilight brings bright tidings which lift sinking spirits. With firm will, I finish climbing, hiking till I find this inviting inn, in which I might sit, dining. I thirst. I bid girls bring stiff drinks —gin fizz which I might sip whilst finishing this rich dish, nibbling its tidbits: ribs with wings in chili, figs with kiwis in icing. I swig citric drinks with vim, tippling kirsch, imbibing it till, giggling, I flirt with girlish virgins in miniskirts: wink, wink. I miss living in sin, pinching thighs, kissing lips pink with lipstick.

Slick pimps, bribing civic kingpins, distill gin in stills, spiking drinks with illicit pills which might bring bliss. Whiz kids in silk-knit shirts script films in which slim girls might strip, jiggling tits, wiggling hips, inciting wild shindigs. Twin siblings in bikinis might kiss rich bigwigs, giving this prim prig his wish, whipping him, tickling him, licking his limp dick till, rigid, his prick spills its jism. Shit! This ticklish victim is trifling with kink. Sick minds, thriving in kinship with pigs, might find insipid thrills in this filth. This flick irks critics. It is swinish; it is piggish. It stinks.

Thinking within strict limits is stifling. Whilst Viking knights fight griffins, I skirmish with this riddling sphinx (this sigil—I). I print lists, filing things (kin with kin, ilk with ilk), inscribing this distinct sign, listing things in which its imprint is intrinsic. I find its missing links, divining its implicit tricks. I find it whilst skindiving in Fiji; I find it whilst picnicking in Linz. I find it in Inniskillin; I find it in Mississippi. I find it whilst skiing in Minsk. (Is this intimism civilizing if Klimt limns it, if Liszt lilts it?) I sigh; I lisp. I finish writing this writ, signing it, kind sir: NIHIL DICIT, FINI.

Lee Ann Brown

Vision Crown
  for James Yamada & Lisa Smith

I sing this Crown of Hymns
  Twined in two leafy wreaths
Come over the sea
  Cross boundary
Sung in these blue mountains

Inlaid with rarest gems
  This garland now will weave
All manner of inspiring fire
  'Tween Heaven and Earthly Love

Crown them with Fiery Crowns
  As Double Helix turns
The vortex of
This Wondrous Love
  Forever more will burn

Abundance of our Love
  We gather here today
The ever-widening fiery Spheres
  Together let us say:

Crown them with many Crowns
  A Crown is like a Ring
That circles round us all in turn
  And sings and sings and sings:

Be Thou My Vision
O Love of my Heart
Naught be all else to me
Save that thou Art

My own true Love
By day or by Night
Waking or Sleeping
Thy Vision my Light

Institutional Velvet

cold halls   begotten / relish
                                        whether

What faults he had
(For who from faults is free?)

blight with plague this marriage hearse

no tolerance for alcohol

            suppose to be

Actual Honey

Planet Saturn turns
    baby rick rack
so fetching against a tourniquet bib

It hurts so quirky
Patchwork mind out on a limb

as bland as pink woolen footies

No   Matter   What
Only Touch the Front

Art impoverished

   a starving lullaby

Hello little baby
I am the Mother

The Ballad of Amiri B. (60's)

Once was a man
     Name of Leroi Jones
To be a culture worker
     In his bones

Down into the South
     Drove the coastline
Said this country
     Ain't no way all mine

Charleston was a sauna
     No sign of breeze
Even though he prayed
     Couldn't even breathe

Went to Ol' Miss
     To look on Faulkner's grave
Said *Ash to Ash man*
     Look who's the slave

Old man he said
     Better look see
Your most intimate photo
     Is history

Baraka: Blessed Amiri
　　Only stayed with his,
Signifying strongly
　　All the unfinished biz

Wouldn't talk to white boys
　　Larry F. and Allen G.
Even though they used to keep
　　Company

But Larry told the tale
　　As the subway flashed by
Amiri gave us whiteboys
　　A wink of his eye

Ben Marcus

The Name Machine from Notable American Women

I'll not be able to list each name we called my sister—the process would
be exhausting, requiring me to relive my sister's pitiful life, and there are
additionally copyright issues connected with persons that are officially the
holdings of the government, which is still the case with my sister, despite her
demise. To reproduce the precise arc of names that she traversed during
her life in our "house" would be to infringe on a life-narrative owned by the
American Naming Authority. It will suffice to select those names sufficiently
resonant of her, that still seem to speak of the girl she was rather than of
some general American female figure, although it could be argued that we
can no longer speak with any accuracy of a specific person, that the specific
person has evolved or lapsed and given way to the general woman, distinguished primarily by her name.

The names defined here derive from a bank of easily pronounceable
and typical slogans used to single out various female persons of America and
beyond. A natural bias will be evident toward names that can be sounded
with the mouth. The snap, clap, and wave, while useful and name like in
their effect (the woman or girl is alerted, warned, reminded, soothed), are
generally of equal use against men, and therefore of little use here. Gestures
of language that require no accompanying vocal pitch, such as gendered
semaphore, used in the Salt Flats during the advent of women's silent
television, or Women's Sign Language (WSL), developed in the 70's as a
highly stylized but difficult offshoot of American Sign Language, now nearly
obsolete because of the strenuous demands it placed upon the hips and
hands—were never successful enough with my sister to warrant inclusion
in the study. She plainly didn't respond to the various postures and physical attitudes we presented to her—our contortions and pantomime proved
not theater enough to distract her into action. No shapes we made with
our hands could convince her that there was important language to be had
in our activity, and she often sat at the window waiting for a spoken name,
without which she could not begin the task of becoming herself.

This is certainly not to imply that "communication" between persons
and living things requires tone or sound, or that deaf figures of the female
communities can have no names. There is always written text, to be appre-

hended through visual or tactile means, as well as the German-American technique of "handling" or squeezing the name of a woman onto her thigh, a formalized body language, which when spoken against a girl is considered a vote of confidence—"I believe in you"—although an adult woman might find the contact to be patronizing. My sister, as it happens, did not respond in any useful way to our repeated and varied handling of her body. As rough as we were, it made no apparent impression on her.

Here the American female name is regarded as a short, often brilliant word. Rarely should it inaccurately capture the person it targets, and its resistance to alternate uses, modifications, translations, and disruptions is an affirmation that individuals can and should be entirely defined by a sharp sound out of the mouth—these definitions have simply yet to be developed and written. Once they are, we will know what there is to know about all future persons who take on one of the appellations listed in the American Bank of Names, striving in their own particular way to become women of distinction.

Nicknames, admittedly, allow for a broader range of fetching, commanding and calling, but the nickname only indicates an attribute or device of a person, such as the length of her legs, the way she sleeps, how she bounces a ball (in this case: Sticks, Taffy, Horse). A name, as the government instructs, can no longer be an accessory of a person but must be her key component, without which the person would fold, crumble. She would cease, in fact, to be a person. The nickname, and more particularly the endearment (honey, doddy, love, lady), speak to a deeper mistrust of the original name, a fear of acknowledging the person at hand. If it is possible to change a person by changing her name, why not employ a name of diminished potential and thus diminish or destroy the person? It's a valid concern. When a man modifies or adorns a woman's name, or dispatches an endearment into her vicinity, he is attempting at once to alter and deny her, to dilute the privacy of the category she has inherited and to require that she respond as someone quite less than herself. (Conversely, women who are scared of their own names are also typically afraid of mirrors). The movement toward a single name for the entire female community (Jill, James, Jackie)—as aggressively espoused by Sernier and practiced by his younger employees—would disastrously limit the psychological and emotional possibilities for women and, rather than unify "them" as the Bible claims, probably force a so-called girl's war in their ranks, in which a large and cancerous body reduces itself into oblivion.

The task of my "family" in this regard was to process and unravel the names that arrived in the mail, then dispatch them onto my sister, generally with the naming bullhorn, a small seashell my mother carved for the purpose. We were enlisted by the government to participate in what was being called the most comprehensive book ever attempted, a study meant to catalog the names of American women. In the book, each name is followed by a set of tendencies that are certain to arise if the user employs the name as the full-time slogan for herself. The book is meant to serve as a catalog of likely actions, to not only predict various future American behaviors, but to control them. If the government regulates the demographics of name distributions, using a careful system of quotas, it can generate desired behaviors in a territory as well as prevent behavior that does not seem promising. It's not exactly a style of warfare as much as it is deep dramatic control over the country. The book remains unpublished, but its authors are reported to be numerous, somewhere in the thousands, each working blind to the efforts of the others. In my possession are only the notes taken during the naming experiments on my sister—an intuitive set of definitions of the names she inhabited. We were not instructed how to define the names we were given, only to "use" them, study them, employ whatever research we could devise. I therefore have no notion if our material was ever incorporated into the text. We submitted it promptly, but never received word on the matter.

We served up the names to my sister one by one and watched her change beneath them. Researchers here might say that she became "herself" or that it was her body expressing its name, as if something does not know what it is until the proper sound is launched at it. Each new morning that she appeared before us and we announced the name for the day through the bullhorn, we saw her become the new girl and release the old one, drop the gestures and habits and faces that the last name had demanded of her and start to search for the necessities of the new name.

I presume that other men launch their childhoods with sticks and mitts and balls, skinned knees, a sock full of crickets, and other accessories. They are shoved onto a lawn where they know the routine, can find the snake or book of matches, sniff out water, or sit in a children's ditch and "watch" the sky with their light and delicate heads. But I was the designated writer among us, unable to walk across grass or throw or catch or hide, equipped only with the stylus and pad, made to create our life in the form of notes on a page. This was unfortunate, because I don't like to write, I don't like to read, I like language itself even less. My "father" read to me as a boy and I was mannered enough not to stop him. It was unbearable—book after book that failed to make or change me, my father's lips twisting and stretching during a supposed "story" hour, massaging a stream of nonsense inside his mouth. I have always tried to be polite about words—good manners are imperative in the face of a struggling father wrestling with a system that has so clearly failed—yet I find language plainly embarrassing. It is poor form, bad manners, that so much hope is pinned to such wrong sounds out of the mouth, to what is really only a sophisticated form of shouting and pain. It is not pleasant for me to hear "foreign" languages, either. All languages are clearly alien and untrue, and absent of so-called meaning it is repeatedly clear that language is a social form of barely controlled weeping, a more sophisticated way to cry. To speak is to grieve, and I would prefer not to listen to a weeping animal all day and every day, sobbing and desperate and lost. Particularly when that animal calls itself my father.

Each time we changed my sister's name she shed a brittle layer of skin. The skins accrued at first in the firewood bin and were meant to indicate something final of the name that had been shed—a print, an echo, a husk, although we knew not what. They were soft in my hands, devoid of information and quite like what I always thought was meant by a "blanket," a boy's little towel, something to shield me from the daily wind that got into my room. It is not that the skins resembled a person any more, or stood for one, or acted as a map of the past. They were rather a part of my sister I could have to myself—soft, foldable, smelling of bitter soap, perhaps like a toy she might have used. I kept them for hand warmers, penciled my pictures into their flaky surfaces, draped them over my bedroom lamp for spidered lighting effects and the whiff of a slightly burnt wind. Maybe I smelled something deeper as the skins burned away on the bulb, floating in and out of the cone of light that enabled my infrequent passage from bed to door, at such times when my bedpan was full. There was nothing of food to the smell, only houses, hands, glass and hair. And her. They smelled of her.

Oddly, these skins my sister shed seemed to serve as a repellant to my sister herself, as if smelling her own body was uncomfortable for her. She would not come near my room when I was using them. Nor would she approach me, particularly if I wrapped myself in parts of her old body and walked through the halls, or bathed in a caul of her husks, which would cling to my skin in a gluey callus when they were wet. No one, I would venture, likes to be understood as deeply as I was understanding my sister at that time, shrouding myself in the flakes of her body that she had lost, wearing her. She preferred, I assume, not to know me.

When the names ran dry, my sister pulled up short somewhere in the heart of the Learning Room. The mail had ceased and no one was sure what to call her. She slept on the rug and scratched at herself, looking desperately to all of us for some sign of a new name, of which we had none. No one, as I mentioned, was sure what to call her, a problem that proved to be the chief void in her identity, which slowly eroded into nothing. There were no more skins, and one morning my sister lost her motion and folded into a quiet pose. Out of sympathy, we reverted back to her original name, or one of the early ones. I have to admit that I'm not sure what name she began with. Nor were any of us too sure, to be frank, who exactly she had become.

[Lisa]

Because the word "Lisa" most closely resembles the cry heard within the recorded storms at the American Weather Museum, a crisply distorted utterance claimed to be at the core of this country's primary air storms, the girl or woman to carry the burden of the Lisa name carries also perhaps the most common sound the world can make, a sound that is literally in the air, everywhere and all the time. (Most wind, when slowed down, produces the sound "Lisa" with various intonations). The danger is one of redundancy, and furthermore that a woman or girl cruelly named "Lisa" will hear her name so often that she will go mad or no longer come when called. Children learn that repeating a word makes it meaningless, but they don't know why. Briefly: Weather in America occurs through an accumulation and disturbance of language, the mildest form of wind. To speak is to create weather, to supply wind from a human source, and therefore to become the enemy. The female Silentists are silent primarily to heal the weather, or to prevent weather, since they believe that speech is the direct cause of storms and should forever be stifled. A Silentist regards the name Lisa as the purest evil, given that, when heard, it commonly indicates an excess of wind, an approaching storm, possibly the world storm. The word "Lisa," to some

Americans, is more dangerous than the words "fuck" or "fag" or "dilch." It should probably be discontinued. It can crush someone.

> *Statistics for Lisa:* An early name of my sister. She rarely acknowledged it. It caused her anger. We could pin her to the floor with it. She drank Girls' Water and would peaceably wear a Brown Hat. Her Jesus Wind resistance was nearly zero. Rashes and facial weakness were frequent. A distressed tone to her skin. Her language comprehension was low, or else she showed selective deafness. A growling sound was heard when she wrote. She seemed blind to my father.

[Erin]

The Erin is a key girl in many American houses. It is often misnamed Julie, Joanne, or Samantha, and sometimes it is clothed as a man. As a man, it is still beautiful, although less visible, and prone to lose color during sleep. It makes love and has slender legs, while persons that see it are eager to palm the spot where the woman parts would be, to sweep and pan their hands over the heat of the man that is hiding her. Persons pry a finger into its mouth and feel weak and sweet in the legs, deriving pleasure through this gateway into Erin, breaking through the husk of a man's body into an inner body named Erin, sometimes breaking past that also to touch at the smooth core and stain their hands on it. There are text versions of Erin as well. Reading them is similar to seeing Erin. It takes a day to read the full version of Erin and the process is exhausting. The text cannot be memorized and sometimes the ending comes abruptly and frightens the reader. The first lusciously bright pile of Erin, that the others feed from, is located in Denver and kept warm by a man named Largeant. It must be swallowed quickly or it will cut and wound the mouth.

> *Statistics for Erin:* My sister refused all clothing but an old, beige throw rug. She crawled around under the rug, but mostly at night. No real language was exhibited, though she made rudimentary attempts at Burke. She seemed concerned to exhibit clean geometries with her body beneath the rug: circles, triangles, squares. We could not get her to wear a sleep sock. If she fainted, she did so without our knowledge.

[Tina]

The Tina will die. It will emerge in Chicago and reside in chipped white houses of wood and warped glass. It will die quietly. When it does not emerge in Chicago there will be something uncertain and weak to its shape, a rough tongue, and hair that a father has unjustly handled. It will die on a Tuesday and the hands will go blue. There is promise to the newer Tina shape. It is blackened through ancestral practice, but can be watery in color and always toughly full. There is a milky storm nearby this Tina figure, and girl versions often dive into the heart of the wind for cleansings. Nothing by way of an answer is ever found in it. On its back is a mark, a freckle, a blister, a scar.

> *Statistics for Tina:* My sister walked upright and spoke basic English. Her face approximated gestures of "happiness." Her nocturnal actions were mostly low-level postures of sleep. Excellent wind resistance. She showed confusion when we stopped calling her Tina. She had already decorated some of her belongings with this name.

[Patricia]

It isn't the most willing shape to swim or lunge or use force to motion over the road. The body prefers the easiness of a chair and a stick to point at what it likes. It is most fully in the Patricia style in the evenings, with brittle hairings and admirable mouth power. They have a Patricia everywhere now, sometimes many. There is no conflict in an abundance of it, which can be considered the chief difficulty. There are many and yet it seems as though there are none. It will be born in America and will exist most successfully as a child. Often, though, the Patricia system lives well into the last posture before demise, beyond the view of childhood. Age falls all over her and makes her walk down into the ground and sleep as though she lived in a grave. She calls out from her grave phone but the ringing sounds only like a dog sleeping and is ignored. It is then allowed to witness itself as an earlier thing, a thing best seen young. The older Patricia fights off the young girl Patricia. It will kill it down again and again, achieving nothing, but killing it nevertheless, creating space for something else that is new and wildly bodied. The young Patricia eats a large bowl of corn for pleasure. It weeps at the sight of water.

Statistics for Patricia: My sister was mostly pliant as Patricia. She willingly posed in several behavior statues for my mother. No resistance to the Brown Hat, which allowed her to converse fluently with several of my mother's assistants. They spoke a language that sounded like slow laughter.

[Carla]

There are fabrications that go forth under the Carla tag. They are smallish and brown-hued. There is an actual Carla at a school and it will learn to beat away the fake occasions of its own number. It will see one coming up the road, one little brown Carla, with fingers like American bread and a hairdo cut right out of the afternoon. The real Carla circles the false object and places fire on its living parts. Many times an American fire contains glittered fragments of a combusted Carla. There are fires in Ohio and girls are leading their dead parts into them. Every morning in every city young women are seen chancing a look back down the road. Sometimes a sluggish fat-skinned fake is sulking back there, waiting to take over and fail in Carla's place. When the Carla makes comfort with boys under trees and farther out on the landscape, there is an apology to the movement of its hands. It touches a boldly upright kid's penis and then palms the dust, the soot, the soil, feeling for the tremor of legs approaching.

Statistics for Carla: A name regularly used on my sister. She showed frequent bloating, and could not fit into the sleep sock. A Ryman Sock was used with much discomfort. Her evening mimes were striking as Carla. Often she could calm the entire household.

[Nancy]

I saw one at a bed. It kneeled, it leaned. There was hair and a body and no such thing as weather, no window broken onto a wall, nor water rushing behind us, or a road to remind me I could leave. Something like this is waiting to happen for everyone. A room somewhere sweetened with a Nancy system. You can approach it and examine its teeth. They are the color of an old house and have chewed their way through something—a trap, a net, a man's hand. I let my arms operate like they did when I was a little boy. I "held" it. It did not bite, it did not speak. I stumbled. It gestured for me to rest. The Nancy shape cannot be detached from the woman it stands for. It can be released, to drag a bed—from a rope looped over its hips—into the city, putting to sleep the visitors that approach her and speaking to them certain facts, certain secrets as they dream, until they can rise from the sheets and move away from her into the distance, toward an area lacking all Nancy, dull and shoe-colored and simple, an American city with other kinds of "people," and life beyond restriction.

> *Statistics for Nancy*: No skin was shed after my sister used this name. My father repeatedly scoured her skin with the pelt brush, to no avail. The only language she exhibited was to say "Nancy" until she collapsed with fatigue. A highly harmful name. Possibly a harmful word. None of us enjoyed calling her this.

[Julie]

There is probably no real Julie.

[Linda]

From 1984 until the Winter of 1987 an absence of significant registered Lindas spurred a glut of naming activity in that category, by parents eager to generate unique-seeming figures into the American landscape and thus receive credit for an original product, the Linda. The resulting children are emerging mostly out of Virginia, with a possible leader, or group of leaders, working through Richmond. Examples have been seen in the West—small and shockingly white with delicate eyes—but they have been poor in health and have not lasted. Weather cuts them down and hides their life until it is too late, and they die. Sometimes rain is blamed. Sometimes nothing but wind. The adult community—too old to register their names and therefore unable to receive the benefits of official status—has nevertheless been supportive of the surge. The tall and stately Lindas, with plenty of money and a husband, have politely vacated their homes, allowing the new Linda-children in for full access to their men, their things, their lives. The older ones enter a sack and wait.

> *Statistics for Linda*: High-level exhaustion during the Linda phase. My sister showed bewilderment and frequently made evasive maneuvers. Quick on her feet and difficult to catch. Often we could not find her. She seemed frequently inclined to play dead. A non-useful name for her. Highly inaccurate. May have caused permanent damage.

[Deborah]

There are about fifty known pure examples of it in the Rocky Mountain area, some dating as far back as 1931. They are thought to improve the people they encounter. The usual number of finished girls in a territory as common as "Deborah" is twenty-eight, with a quota of twenty and a maximum limit of thirty-two. Any more than this should suggest a dilution of the original Deborah, which produces strains of Amy or Ellen. Although the mid-century Rocky Mountain persons had utilized a Deborah to comfort the saddest local families, reserving the medical Deborah for only the most dangerous cases of grief, the need for a cheer-spreading personage began to be felt at a national level and abductions and faking occurred. There is consequently an extreme Deborah in the East, possibly of Colorado origin but bred through men of the Mid-west (and therefore tall and reddish and chalky), dispensing a form of nearly unbearable, radical happiness into cities and homes. It is often housed in a little body, but its range is wide and its effect is lasting. To say "Deborah" is to admit to sadness, and ask for help.

> *Statistics for Deborah*: She preferred modifications to her head when we called her this. No matter how far we launched her in the chair, my sister did not faint. Small emotional showings were on view: contentment and pleasure, occasional cheer. She attempted to embrace my mother, usually before bedtime, and my mother only barely escaped these approaches. Sometimes she endured long hugs from this Deborah.

[Susan]

From afar, the Susan appears to be buckling, shivering, seizing, its body exhibiting properties of a mirage. Up close, there is mass to Susan and it is real to the touch. There will be food for you if you are Susan, although possibly a pile of food for Susan is a trap, to be regarded with suspicion. It is an elegant and refined system that established a school for itself, The Susan House. Its doctrine, The Word of Susan, is useful also to versions of Julia and Joyce but can be harmful to Judith. All of its books have gone unwritten.

> *Statistics for Susan*: Quite poor weather during this phase. My sister aged considerably and showed signs of acute attention and superiority. In-

sisted on privacy. Dressed formally. Seemed not of our family. Our presence confused her. She once asked my father how he knew her name. My father could not answer her.

[Jesus]

Women achieve their Jesus by speaking and studying their own name. The original Jesus figure examined his name, then derived actions and strategies from his analysis. This is the primary purpose of the Jesus noise—self-knowledge, instruction, advice. Women betray their Jesus when they forget that there is an answer at the heart of their name, to be divined or surmised by loud, forceful recitations of it in the streets, for as long as it takes. Simply saying "Jesus," however, is ineffective. (Breathing is the most common strategy for remembering our names).

> *Statistics for Jesus*: It was decided not to call my sister this. Mother felt we might lose her. But I tried it anyway one night when my parents were asleep. I had to use a low volume setting on the naming bullhorn and I whispered it at her while she slept. It was during an early Tina phase. She never woke. I sat at her bed all night and used this name against her until my mouth was exhausted. Nothing happened.

[Father]

To refer to a woman as "Father" is to engage her inner name and fill her hands with power. It is a code that many American women respond to with energy and hope. It is therefore used as a healing noise, particularly at hospitals, where the word "Father" is uttered by nurses to women who are ill or tired. When men make love to "Father" they use hearty motion and often call out words of labor and ecstasy; they thank Father, and they ask Father for more. Men in Utah, where this sort of naming is most frequent, take Father to the baths and hold her while rinsing her hair until she feels soothed and calm, until she is manageable and not crazy with power, or too big for her body, or at least not dirty and alone, which makes Father dangerous. In wealthy households, Father enters a boy's room and blackens it with a gesture of her hand, then starts in on the boy with warm oil on his thighs, squeezing the oil into his legs until he weeps or breathes easy. Father pulls back the sheets and she climbs in to treat the boy and teach him to live. A boy often first makes love to Father because she is gentle and confident, someone the boy can trust. He holds onto Father's hands when she straddles the bed and effects her graceful motion. A boy says "Father" as she leans over him to help, dipping and rising, although sometimes the boy is quiet, preferring to feel her deepening attentions and not destroy the moment with speech.

Statistics for Father. Chaos at the house. My real father was banished during this phase. He slept in the shed. I wanted to call him a girl's name, but I was not allowed to see him. My sister clearly thrived as Father: she boomed, she boasted, she tore through the house. She smashed the behavior television, she burned her old sleep sock. Mother was scared. A soothing litany of vowel songs were used on my sister to calm her down, without which she may have escaped. By the time the name would have worn off, she would have reached Akron. We restricted the study to two days. When we stopped calling her father, she shed the hardest skin of all the names. My mother removed it from the house before inviting my father back inside.

[Mary]

Every five minutes, a woman named Mary will stop breathing. It is a favorite of children and every five minutes there are children standing in witness to the ending of Mary. Children clap at it when they see it. They are thrilled and they weep. Sometimes they become excited by a Mary that comes to die before them and they chase it and hit it. The Mary takes a wound. It holds up an arm and shields what is coming. It holds a wound in its hand and the children are delighted.

Statistics for Mary. She was mostly slumped over. This was near the end. We tried to groom her, but her body was cold. Her hair broke when you touched it. She weakened visibly everytime we said Mary. She refused all food. In the mornings, she wrung her hands and wept quietly. Mother collected something from her face. Possibly some scrapings, possibly the smallest bit of fluid. Mary was the last thing we called her. It was possibly the name that killed her.

[...]

Certain factions of women go by a non-name and therefore participate in a larger person that is little seen or heard or known. It cannot be summoned or commanded. Generally it walks stiffly, owing to its numerous inhabitants. A body such as one not named can be toppled no doubt—felled and pinned to the turf, brought under control with water and a knife, some rope, and hard words. It is the primary woman from which many women have emerged, to which many will return. It is believed to reside in Cleveland. Probably it is bleeding and tired. By now it might be nearly finished.

> *Statistics*: We treated my sister with silence at the end. If there was a name that meant "good-bye," that is what I would have called her. If there was a name that meant "I'm sorry." If there was a name to get her back.

continued

Anna Maria Maiolino: A Life Line/Vida Afora

January 15, 2002

Rod Smith
Nada Gordon and Gary Sullivan
Charles Bernstein

*This reading followed an indirect tack, using some of the major stops along Maioli-
no's conceptual and literal path as ways to imagine analogies in poetry. Maiolino
was born in 1942 in Calabria, Italy, and settled in Rio de Janiero, Brazil, in 1960,
where, moving from Italian to Portuguese, she was forced to work in a new language.
As Catherine de Zegher has suggested, language and its displacement have become, for
Maiolino, associated with a version of materiality—both physical and sonic. In the
sixties and seventies, Maiolino made "mental maps" that knowingly reduced complex
geographical and social displacements into pseudo-systematic illustrations: they linked
and systematized the unlinkable. This tendency to figure displacements as potentiali-
ties rather than absences is characteristic of Maiolino's larger critique of the poetics
of loss developed by many Modernist artists and writers. Maiolino's work instead,
especially in her thread-based studies, uses activities such as stitching to explore
multi-layered metaphors of connectivity. Threaded nodes and linked points also turn
abstract lines and planes into material objects. This recasting of representation's basic
materials pushes the graphic into the context of the sculptural.*

*The three poets in this reading also look (paradoxically) toward the basic resources of
their medium in order to push it into new contexts. I want to concentrate on sound
play as a way to focus this process—since it is at once a fundamental element of poetry
and also a potentially (and fruitfully) disruptive force, puncturing fixed semantic
contexts by extending "inappropriate" semantic links or sonic threads. Framing
a string of oblique, disjunctive often sound play-based poems in terms of personal
names—Larry, Bert, Mel, Woodward—Rod Smith's "The Boy Poems" in* Protective
Immediacy *improvise on and compellingly distort the basic descriptive and narrative
units of biographical writing. "The Classics" develops a similar discrepancy between
titles from canonical works of theory and philosophy and contingently related poems.
In both one thus reads the titles and names in terms of the poems and vice versa, experiencing a charged gap that sometimes suddenly disappears as the theory and poem,
or name and description, briefly share a possible horizon. This sudden and humorous
flickering into focus of two ostensibly distant objects is an effect we might associate
with homophonic translation when the translation, just a second ago miles away in
sound play, suddenly seems to touch or comment directly on its source text. This points
to how the conceptual structures important to Smith's books are never independent of
a second-to-second sound exploration. Or better, heightened attention to sound itself
becomes a basic condition in which conceptual structures operate: "my bee beheld egg-
head star demon stuff like usual." In his most recent book,* The Good House, *which*

explores the spatial, social, moral, and sentimental categories people use to explain the concept of home to themselves, these conceptual structures are also literal structures— houses—which then become special sites for identification with the material world, for hope in the inhuman as, hopefully, a kind of investment in the human.

The singular and then plural conditions of Nada Gordon's coming to live in Brooklyn with the poet Gary Sullivan make up the story of Swoon. *The book thus falls into the rapidly emerging genre of the email epistolary romance, though it is also an encyclopedic work. It contains, among many other currents, accounts from Gordon, who was living in Tokyo, of that city's commutes, floor mats, and food, and descriptions from Sullivan, who was living in Brooklyn, of that borough's bars, apartments, and poet constellations; a poetry and theory anthology (of the two poets' works, as well as works by Laura Riding, Robert and Elizabeth Barrett Browning, and Roland Barthes); a treatise (several treatises, really) on interpretation in general and on the poets' own works in particular; holograph reproductions of letters, photos, and cartoons; and a collection of theoretical and quite practical texts on relationships, love, sex—on horizons of expectation—and some porno, to boot. How many other currents there were to this life-consuming and life-generating correspondence we do not know, as the book makes up just over 300 pages from the 5,000 pages exchanged. Such volume—the enthusiasm, detail, and love projected by and in it—created an actual life context as well as a wonderful book. And in so doing the work both falls into and provides new terms for a long line of avant-garde experimentation that emerges necessarily from the gap between resolutely non-art-based lived experience and literature. As Chris Stroffolino points out in his afterword, "Love is not subordinated to the writing, but neither is the writing subordinated to love."*

It was on Charles Bernstein's "Poetics List" that Gary and Nada met, making Bernstein a significant...precondition for this couple. Bernstein's status as a precondition, and as an impetus, can of course be extended into much contemporary poetry and poetics. For instance, the sound generation we see in Rod Smith and the literal song we hear in Nada Gordon both relate to Bernstein's practice of evoking and deforming the structures of children's and rhyming poetry. These deformations misquote poetry back to itself as a structure of sound-patterned language at the same time as they incorporate idiolects, overheard speech, clichés, aphorisms, and graphic stutters—opening verse language to areas of quotidian life and culture from which it is usually held at a distance. And it is perhaps these linkages—in which Bernstein uses poetry's history of

sound play to connect it (without apology, solemnity, or predictability) to an expand-
ing territory—that suggest analogies with Maiolino's poetics of connectivity, where
fissures in the materiality of paper open the usual plane of absent representation onto
modes of three-dimensional enactment. —LS

Rod Smith
from *The Good House*

anything can be made out of a house.

though many of them are blue.

there's a kind of recovery in it then.

too much innocence, or minutes
left out, those.

a time, or economic worry, a
weird abreaction.

seeps
in the house are loans one cannot trust.

a trusted house, the work of
the house, a dirigible.

seeps in the house should not be imagined.

———

the worst is not good, it's alone & not nourish

———

time is a housed reputable beginner

thirty more are needed

tripping, the house kneads the flower,
spells me, parts the bowl, stuns
& is soft, stuns
& is real

————

the good house is given advice:

In times of danger ceremonious forms are dropped. What
matters most is sincerity.

————

There are 8 houses in the heart,
there should be 9.

————

That it is a house.
That it never moves.
That it loses concentration.
That it questions
& foregoes—does not feel
good—does not
hail—

    half of it, for love

      harbinging

   & voracious
       saplings
    of prayer—
       praying to
  saplings, lots

of lazy, happy, lenient

bested cognizance, the felled

soft letters of coming.

———

the good house—it is heavy,
the good house—it exercises
hope in the inhuman, is transformed
by it—
　　becomes blatant in its strength
　　& is destroyed, the good
　　house must be rebuilt
　　carefully. The good house
　　is in conflict.

———

ordinary houses complete

the smart bombs and are

buoyant—victorious,

brainwaves of shunt commotion,
bestial then or not house

—the load—the
makeup assignment reads long

into the long night, dreams

of lassoes, garbage, things

it thinks it cannot change.

———

if the house were up for rent
things would be different

————

Each reasonable house
& each waking motion
are votive, based on
the wiley resurgence
of awaiting worlds—

————

House & holographic, pastoral
battenings brace
the heart's chosen will
which being one thing,
becomes modest,
plies the decent roads
w/ nests & rope, lone
& casual, available
breezeway of won seeming—
this house, it is
safe & loving, protected
from what is false
unfailing—then no wince
can raise or pillar night
thence town—
        house await
        & house be grown—
        house of house heart
        of house, a lake
        be side, it is sown.

————

Nada Gordon and Gary Sullivan
from *Swoon*

From:	Gary
Date:	December 7
Subject:	12/7

My dear Nada,

        If today I'm as flat as the light on the street below
it is only because I write from great distance, but do curl
as a cover in the sun, toward you, if imperceptibly
wanting more than to be newly come as a first kiss blossoms thick
as summer. I wish today I had its heat, & that heart others "trod on
ages ago," & so this may explain why, yeah, I'm a fool
why the red sun in my throat is yours; well,
it was mine once, now lent to you in utterance, sweet doubt &
scattered brains hacked away to this, my love—but, what point
in bluntness, flat as the light in the street?
                              It's too easy to repeat
& expect subtle difference, nuance; I want every word I do give you
to be new, not newly come. I saw today LOVE: a book of remembrances
& ached we hadn't thought of it (bp Nichol did), it sent me
here, to these words struck against my Underwood "Golden Touch"
's ink-black platen, my cigarettes, & beer as amber as your eyebrows
appear photographed in wiggly fluorescent light, though
they're dark brown, I think, almost black, it's your eyes that
're really amber. & "really real," as Van Morrison would say; & I've got
I realize no right to write you like this, though I don't feel
beguiling, more that you charm vivid color from even this dirty
Brooklyn air. "The year starts in despair/ at ever awakening to it,"
I just bibliomanced, "New Years, Mad," from Coolidge's Solution
Passage, & I wonder at the madness of this, but know equally
I do love you.

It worries me, too, fool that I am, of breaking up
with you into pieces, silent as letters, to be strewn onto water
not able, the winter sun so harsh above the south Brooklyn skyline,
to become, without words, so liquid as this. But this—
imagine foraging for anything like this, among others
more beautiful than us.

That we are not so beautiful is why we may
strive to make this, here—& I mean This, not
these words—so beautiful. Give me Anything & I'll take it
& make of it Everything. For you. What is love if not this promise?
I promise you this: All my promises will be kept, until delivered
& then they will be yours, & what you do with them will be
you. & it's you, that shadow around your mouth, I want. Do you know
what you've done? To me? I drink as the sun sinks below
other projects because I am not, now, drinking you. Only your arms,
your legs, opening, & there you are, you, Nada,
only you wrapped around me, as I am rapt now, thinking of you
matters to me, my hands & arms, lips & tongue useless
that they cannot feel, this moment, how you pulse beneath your skin.
Our cells, the alphabet of our souls.

We will never speak, bodily
in complete sentences, we'll lose every spelling bee, but know
this is only because we did not begin as adults. That's also
"what love is," knowing that, that loveliness is accidental, might
mean a chipped tea cup, flowers oddly situated in a drinking glass
filled with tap water, that nothing might be so perfect
as our seams. Or our "seems," as in "it seems
so perfect on the screen." If you can resist me, in person, if I
fumble lines to your face—elsewhere
"a bee soaked with liquid rises," & that knowledge may be all
that will save us. My only request is that you know
& remember this.

Will to be yourself with me. The sun has just now
disappeared behind white buildings, I need
to do laundry, the everyday seeps in even into this letter, how
keep it out, if I'm to be honest with you? I itch
in my clothes, no doubt reek of cigarettes, beer, sweat & cum
am human & animal as you are human & animal
should boil tea to sober up, begin to think "How can I quit smoking?"
How can I do laundry, having written you this? I close
my eyes, having stared at this photograph of you too long,
it soothes nothing, I know I'll wake tomorrow, my extremities cold
my thoughts curled in your syntax, my body still quick w/your
image, it was somewhat cruel of you to send me such beautiful photos
don't you think? Or not cruel, but beguiling, as if to say
"I'm yours," when, no, you're there, I hope we can forgive each other
knowing cruelty as a product of distance.

       My mouth feels like it just
fell off, I lift my beer to it but there's only my tongue
& this, my language is what you've reduced me to, or elevated me towards, as though writing you were loving you, which it is, but
no it's not; Nada, I want, need, to love you, bodily & soulfully, meaning
bodily over time. Deny me that & I will sink back w/fits suspended
against my face, my tongue will grow dim, my arms will rest
as fallen dominoes. I write this as the sky grows purple
& paper dim.

       Whatever happens, Nada, I know we will never again
imagine our skin to be protective. I know, too
what insomnia is, & that love is not merely attendance. It's also sound
that numbs logic. It's this neighborhood we live in. It's whatever story
you tell me that I relive.

The ruckus of this letter is no accident
it's how my very words love you. It's how vain I feel
feeling the sun exists to warm me. "From letter distance I am made,"
only I'm here now, seeping nitrogen, able only to light
another match, able only to confront all the things I think
looking at your photograph. What, I dread, will we become
if not together? "Understanding"? That's the last thing
any bruised heart hopes for. Mine, or yours. "Let all our mistakes
be jewels," our sparks & low grunts no relief. I will never
ever, be "relieved of" you. You're too deeply inscribed. No one,
my love, will ever write you like this, no words this
insectile, no letter so porous. Reading this, you reading this,
I know, & do feel, you seep. We are not poor in spirit. & so,
let us no longer starve for love,

                        Gary

From: nada
Date: December 8
Subject: Lubricity

ohhh ...

liquid butter and
totally green
stockings

when i think of you
i think of dope

this is the line
that built the ray
that juts out of the stratosphere

a maze

at you   in you   around you

*

looking for silky, for silky...
sweep
or the glue
with glitter in it

feel it. sense it.
savor it.
taste it.

immediately.

or put on your fedora
and go outside,
to think

*

in optic fiber
on dizzying satellites
there were rhapsodists kissing

(in letters)
insects
singing outside
(I want to sing outside)

and time
time is totally
glue

did you notice
how i wrote you into life?

the twitching
life
our writing
made? twinkling
the colloquial…

*

cypresses.
daisies.
pines, pining.
pine box.
plastic box's
circuits > > > > >
our nerves…

be still my mind

pressure at the temples

the tree of life
droops over
an engraving
of a couple

below whom
an axiom (epigram)
makes total sense

time is totally
cyclone.

now that you're here
you might as well
lie down
with
me
.

.

.

we might hold up our hands
in gratitude
for the godz
to rain down
miniature cherries,
weeping dwarf red
cedar, weeping
fig, wooly thyme,
marigolds, beauty
secrets, anemones,
pygmy bamboo,
indoor landscapes

waltzing like
infants
praying like
telephones
                like modems,
like telephones

*

poetry, then
has some efficacy

a poem
whose only word is
SWOON

*

this lyricism
is a kind of
blood, or
oil, or
semen, or
sand

and it keeps on pouring out
its lubricity
beyond quandary

the camellia[‡]
a vulva
after all

> [‡]open, inviting, pinkish, dewy

Charles Bernstein

Anaffirmation

I am not I
when called to account –
plaster over, dumbly benched
the corrosive ardency
of blinkered identification.
To affirm nothing, a veil
of asymptotic bent,
prattling over-
tunes in the striated
ecstasy of an turned-
around spade. Sprain parkway
gulls its titular
horizon, & my growling
Zebra knows me just
enough to tip
her hat.

Thinking I Think I Think

What are aesthetic values and why do
there appear to be lesser & fewer of
them? Quick: define the difference
between arpeggio & Armani. The baby
cries because the baby likes crying.
The baby cries because a pin is
sticking into the baby. The baby
is not crying but it is called
crying. Who's on first, what's
shortstop. The man the man declined
to be, appraised at auction at
eighty percent of surface volume.
Cube steak on rye amusing twist
on lay demo cells, absolutely no

returns. *Damaged goods are the only
kind of goods I ever cared about.*
The lacuna misplaced the ladle,
the actor aborted the fable. Fold
your caps into Indians &
flaps. Dusting the rigor mortis
for compos mentis. Rune is busting
out all over – perfidious quarrel
sublates even the heckling at
the Ponderosa. A bevy of belts.
Burl Ives turned to burlap. Who
yelled that? Lily by the lacquer
(laparotomy). *I'm here strictly on
business, literary business.* May
I propose the codicil-ready cables?
Like slips gassing in the night.
Chorus of automatic exclusions.
Don't give me no label as long as I
am able. Search & displace, curse
& disgrace. Suppose you suppose,
circumstances remonstrating. Crest
envy. Don't give me the Bronx
when you mean the Bronx. *This
one thing I know for she loathes
me so:* Ketchup will pass for blood
only under highly limited conditions.
I had a red ball / I watched it
fall. *Help me so that I may exist
again.* It's the billyclub not the
Billy that needs watching. Keep
your eye on the balloon (cartoon)!
Budge, but then move back into
position. In other words, steal
my car but don't steal my sister's
hood. Ironclad comeuppance. Breakfast
at the Eiffel tower, lunch at the
Kremlin, dinner at the Taj Mahal.

In other words, *hurt me*
but don't hurt me so bad.
May flies / So June can hold
July. That's no arrow that's a
diversionary tactic. That's no
spastic that's my elocutionary
lodge. When all the cares
have become little tiny porous
creatures, buckling under the weight
of the remorse. The barfly butters
his bread on all sides of the
collective agency, while even at home
the Colonel takes out the garbage.
You will find a moist towelette
with your porridge. Then just say so.
Cratylus, Cratylus, wilt thou be
mine? As I is the starch from
yesterday's yawning. Cure me
so that I will smoke yet not be
consumed (at least not at a
discount). *Pools rush in*
where barriers have not been
fortified. Rule rules
where furriers redesign. "Amish
modern." French poetry is looking
for a way out of "French poetry".
Ne touchez pas cette button. The
color of baloney. WWW.TheSirens.Org.
Ne touchez pas ma bologna. Her
hair was auburn her eyes like amber.
Honest to gosh gullies: arraignment
of a power untapped & untappable.
Quittez votre place (Kitaj dislikes
his place). Emboss my fiduciary
capitulations! The bellicose churning
of the unsettled stomach. *National*
Geographic's "Robot" issue:

The Wilderness of the Future, e.g.,
the Gates Robot Preserve, the
American Robotic Conservancy,
the Fund for Robotic Culture,
the National Endowment for Robots
(a.k.a. U.S. Congress). Millions
for automation but not one cent
for elegy. Eight elephants dancing
deliriously to the wail of the
bumble bees. *So long, sailor /
goodbye failure.* Or let the pail
wear the head of the lotion. Here
is smoldering continuation. The
smell of green tea on Greene Street.
Bottled reticence. *Gimme gimme*
gone. Guilt in the form of guilt.
    "& even then my heart was aching
    For I am yours, just for the taking…"

Why We Ask You Not to Touch

Human emotions and cognition

leave a projective film over the poems

making them difficult to perceive.

Careful readers maintain a measured

distance from the works in order

to allow distortion-free comprehension

and to avoid damaging the meaning.

February 19, 2002

Régis Bonvicino *read by* Odile Cisneros
João Cabral de Melo Neto *read by* A. S. Bessa
Cecilia Vicuña

Jumping off from Maiolino's own engagement with Latin American, especially Brazil-ian, poetry, this reading presented the works of two Brazilian poets—Régis Bonvicino (read and introduced by Odile Cisneros) and João Cabral de Melo Neto (read and introduced by A. S. Bessa)—along with the work of the Chilean poet and artist Cecilia Vicuña.

Despite the fact that at least 200 million people speak Portuguese (more than the num-ber who speak French), and despite the fact that Brazilians were among the pioneers of concrete poetry and have had a sequence of extremely significant experimental poetry movements throughout the twentieth century, comparatively little poetry written in Portuguese has been translated into English. In addition to some work translated and anthologized in the context of international concrete poetry, there is Elizabeth Bishop's well-known 1972 anthology, a 1983 anthology by Bishop's co-editor Emanuel Brasil and William Jay Smith, and an anthology from Sun and Moon in 1997. Even at their best, anthologies offer only fragmentary and partial encounters with the authors they include. Full books of poetry by Brazil's most influential poets are almost entirely unavailable in English. Almost nothing, for instance, has been available from Har-oldo de Campos, despite his seminal status in contemporary poetry.

As Odilie Cisnero's brief introduction of Bonvicino, and A. S. Bessa's of Cabral, are presented with the main poetry texts, I will just say a word about Cecilia Vicuña, whose practices as a poet and artist might be taken to parallel and elaborate on some of Maiolino's. In particular, I have in mind the shared interest in a kind of expanded semantics of thread, whose purported expansion is also a return, and a re-examina-tion, of how and what thread has signified both in indigenous South American cultures and elsewhere. Thread for both Vicuña and Maiolino is at once an idea of a link, even a kind of intertextuality, and also a literal, material link, a binding force in three dimensions. One meaning of this materiality for Vicuña has been at the level of words themselves, which she reports experiencing in three dimensions as they open to reveal their inner associations. This experience of the word—externally, spatial-ly—finds a parallel in the American poet Hannah Weiner, whose similar externaliza-tion of words became the basis of her poetics. In Vicuña's writing practice, however, words tend to be linked not so much to constellations of contemporary language as to networks of etymologies and quotations: from Fenollosa, Plato, Maria Sabina, Hera-clitus, Freud, Miguel Leon Portilla, and Heidegger, among others. In works such as

Palabrarmás, *these quotations link a word's synchronic use with its diachronic development, previous uses, and above all for Vicuña, its root. These etymological threads are often organized around a project of recovering fundamental sense perception and, in a way, remaking the world at its most atomic level. It is perhaps this project, then, that might weave Vicuña's interest in weaving into Maiolino's, since both involve a complex and intricate remaking of the world—its textures, patterns, codings, and the intersubjective affiliations brought into being by links inside it. —LS*

Régis Bonvicino

Despite his visible formal indebtedness to Brazilian concrete poetry—a formalist renovation project spearheaded by Haroldo and Augusto de Campos and Décio Pignatari in the fifties and sixties—the early work of São Paulo poet Régis Bonvicino, who was born in 1951, constitutes a departure in many ways, both an assimilation of and a critical dialogue with the devices introduced by the concrete poets. Thematically, the texts focus on the postmodern experience of life in a metropolis such as São Paulo, especially the role of the poet and poetry in the city.

The poem "?avolho" plays on the word "lavolho"—from "lavar" (to wash) and "olho" (eye)—a brand name of eye drops in Brazil, The reference to the language of advertising and the choice of words (a solution used to improve the eye condition) echo concretism's emphasis on visual communication, which is critically undercut by the self-deprecating, ambiguous ending. "Poema resposta comercial" (Poem commercial reply) also plays with non-poetic linguistic conventions. The phrases "não suje/não dobre/ não amasse" (don't soil/ don't fold/ don't wrinkle"), mimic the language of public notices, while "caixa sentimental - n° 1973 - s. paulo - capital" (sentimental mailbox No. 1973, São Paulo), parodies the style of personal ads in newspapers. The whole poem can be read as a meditation on the function of signs and language as impersonal vehicles of private and public urban communication.

"Horreadymades"—a tongue-in-cheek reference to Marcel Duchamp—also deploys the vocabulary and syntax of street signs. The layout, which is responsible for the visual puns that the poems seek to effect, follows concretist notions of the power of graphic space as a textual structuring agent. The three poems can be seen as variations on the same theme. The words "area de segurança" (safety area), "cuidado / obstáculos" (caution / obstacles) and "a 10 cm" (10 cm away), interact with the words/signs "poesia" (poetry), "um poema" (a poem), and "uma palavra" (a word), creating tension in two ways. First, at the semantic level, they emphasize the subversive power of poetry vis-à-vis the modern urban milieu by questioning the established order and anonymity of cities as invoked by traffic signs. Moreover, the poems deconstruct their own structural principle, since the visual puns they seek to effect depend on the humorous juxtaposition of the exclusionary traffic signs and the words "poetry," "a poem," and "a word." The poems acquire a new significance when seen as self-referential, a surprising mise-en-abîme where these very texts are kept at a safe distance, perhaps invoking a different conception of poetry they themselves don't fulfill.

Certain unpalatable factors of city life, such as noise, are present in "oO," which imitates the pulsating Doppler effect of city noises by doubling the letters of the phrase "silence / yells to / forgetfulness / experience / the absurd sound / of a city" in alternating lowercase and uppercase letters. The poem also plays on the similarity of the sounds between the words "olvido" (forgetfulness, oblivion) and "ouvido" (ear, sense of hearing). The humorous use of urban thematic content reveal the poet's empathy with his environment and faith in the regenerative effect of poetry, which are palpably present in "o que há" (what there is). The text plays on the simple rhymes of "alegria/ utopia/ poesia" (joy/ utopia/ poetry), lightheartedly repeating permutations of these combinations and other words. In this optimistic view of the role of poetry as a utopian space, "signs" interact and are equated with "joy," "utopia," and "poetry."

What comes forth from all these poems is that, early on, Bonvicino had critically absorbed the poetic devices of concrete poetry and was ready to employ them, not only as a road to self-expression, but also to attack the possible stagnation that they could lead to. Simultaneously affirming the redemptive power of poetry, Bonvicino 's work points to highly original and viable way out of the concrete jungle.

—Odile Cisneros

Régis Bonvicino

?AVOLHO

?avolho
?av?lho
?av?l?o
?a??l?o
????l?o
??????o
???!???
???o??!

POEMA RESPOSTA COMERCIAL

não suje	não suje
não dobre	não dobre
não amasse	não amasse

não suje	não suje
não dobre	não dobre
não amasse	não amasse

caixa sentimental – nº 1973 – s. paulo – capital

horready mades

área

de

segurança

poesia

a 10 cms.

cuidado

obstáculos

um poema

uma palavra

oO

oO sSilLêÊnNcCiloO

gGrRiItTaA pPaArRaA

oO oOlLvViIdDoO

eExXpPeErRiImMeEnNtTeE

oO aAbBsSuUrRdDoO sSoOmM

dDeE uUmMaA cCiIdDaAdDeE

O QUE HÁ

o que há	o que há	o que há
de alegria	de utopia	de utopia
na poesia	na poesia	na poesia
alegra	alegra	alegra
desperta	desperta	desperta
os signos	os signos	os signos
a utopia	a alegria	a poesia

João Cabral de Melo Neto

João Cabral de Melo Neto (1920–99) belonged to the category of writers who quietly develop their poetic work in the midst of ordinary professional lives. Cabral was a civil servant for his entire life, with a distinguished career in the diplomatic corps.

In the early 1960s, Cabral was appointed head of the Ministry of Agriculture, under the progressive government of João Gullart. After the military coup of 1964, he returned to diplomacy and became the Brazilian consul in Barcelona. Towards the end of his career, he became an ambassador, serving in Senegal and Honduras.

Cabral's poetic project is singular in the context of Brazilian literature. Many see in his poems traces of Surrealism, but I would suggest that his writing tends more toward a kind of "metaphysics of objects," such as we find in the paintings of Morandi, for instance, or Zurbaran.

Many of his poems concern the nature of "things," the materiality of "things," the "presence of thing." He uses simple language and precise images. He is interested in clarity, precision. Yet, some of his images have an enduring, menacing power.

—A. S. Bessa

João Cabral de Melo Neto

For The Book Fair

Leafed through, a book's sheaf retakes
the languid and the vegetal off a leaf's leaf,
and a book is leafed through or left unopened
as, under the wind, the shivering tree;
leafed through, a book's sheaf repeats
fricatives and labials of ancient winds,
and nothing feigns wind on a tree's leaf
better than wind on a book's leaf.
However the leaf, in the book's tree,
more than imitates the wind, proffers
in it word urges voice, which is wind,
or storm sweeping dirt to zero.

*

Silent: be it closed or open,
including the one that screams inside; anonymous:
only the spine exposed on the shelf
that erases in grayness all spines;
modest: it only opens if one opens it,
and as opposed to the painting on the wall
opened all its life, or music,
alive only while its nets fly.
But besides all this, and patiently
(for it allows its reading anywhere), severe:
it demands to be questioned, extracted;
and never exhales: closed, though open.

translated by A. S. Bessa

The Chicken Egg

I

To the eye, an egg shows
the integrity of an object intact.
One matter, unified,
massive egg as a whole.

Without interior and exterior,
such as stones, without innards:
and all innards: interior and exterior
entirely contour.

However, if an egg presents itself unanimous to the eye,
the hand that weighs discovers
in it some suspicious thing.

Its weight is not of a stone,
inanimate, cold, dead;
its weight is warm, tumescent,
live weight, not dead.

II

An egg reveals the finish,
to each caressing hand,
of things well rounded
in the life-long labor

also found in shapes
that hands don't fabricate:
in corals, rolled stones
and many sculpted things
whose simple forms are the work

of a thousand endless chisels
used by sculpting hands
hidden in the water, in the wind.

But, the egg, despite
its final pure form,
is not situated at the end:
it is at the outset.

III

The presence of any egg,
even if the hand won't touch it,
has the gift to instill
a certain reserve in any room.

This is hard to understand
if one thinks of the clear form
an egg holds, and the openness
of its whitewashed wall.

The reserve an egg inspires
is of the scarcest kind
the fear one feels facing a gun
but not facing a bullet.

The fear one feels of things
that conceal something other
and coerce not with a bullet
but just by being loaded

IV

To hold an egg
a ritual is always observed:
there is a reticent way half
religious in those who carry it.

One can pretend that the way
of those who hold any egg
comes from the normal attention of
one who conducts a rounded thing.

The egg, alas, is closed
in its hermetic architecture
and those who hold it, knowing,
persist in the customary rule:

proceed·still in a way
between fearful and circumspect,
nearly beatific, of those who have
in the hands a lit candle.

translated by A. S. Bessa

Buraco Preto / Black Hole

the unspoken field
la parte no hablada
or: my thoughts
as I sing.

rodium → ▢

seats

X

I am in the back row.
They call my name
I don't move

silence
begins

seats

crick crick crick

the rattling sound

the seeds in my hands

these Amazon seeds

(they sound like a crying bird.

that's how you summon them.

I walk the crackling sound,

leaving
my seat

Pulsating
seeds

the room
has a heart?

corazón
y
entraña,
songo?

a
  pentagram
     of thoughts
  the
      seed
          notes

     the death
     of trees

       crying
       seeds.

I reach the podium . I see Maiolino's "Buraco Preto", 1974, to my right.

I say: "all holes are now the hole, ground zero, black hole. Readings cancelled. Do you remember the readings cancelled at the Drawing Center, Sept 11, 2001?

cecilia vicuña

With a Little Notebook at the Met

Talisman

  Would say:
    "writing to be used in the body"
like a talisman
    "the heart of the one who wears it"
the body already a writing
of arteries and veins
  traveling
without end

Thuluth

Neja the form
nema the weft

My lines
have turned into
serpents
and beings
coiling
into each other
their storm

Kufic Writing

Says:
    *"In a Kufic inscription the square grid
    contains the attributes of god."*

The body
twisting

speckled
shadow

a grained
shadowing

Backstitch
on the bias

Neither tone
nor thread
in stead
a sounding.

Linen

Threadiness
of thread

Umbilic
Umbra

The line
is born
from linen

The mother
from the son

Translated by Rosa Alcalá

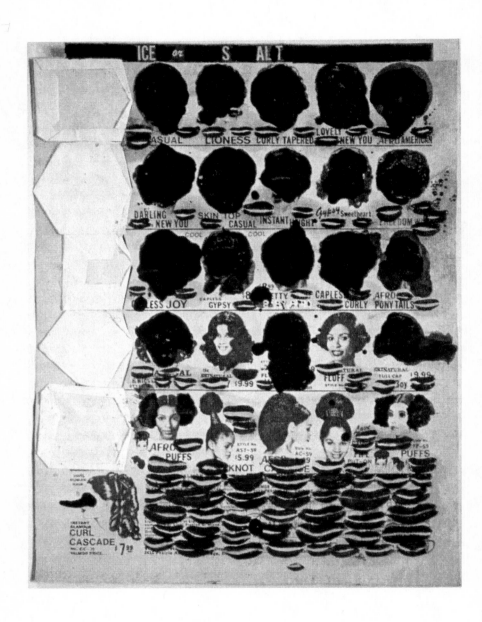

Ellen Gallagher:
Preserve

March 12, 2002

Rachel Levitsky
Edwin Torres
Kevin Young

By marking and refiguring mid-century fashion ads directed at African-Americans, Ellen Gallagher suggests that racial identity, inasmuch as it manifests itself at the level of bodies conditioned by fashion, is a matter of performance. That is, if ads already *produce styles of subjective (though also collective) identity, then their reimagined or defaced language could itself produce others—contestatory, illegible, analytic ones. Thus Gallagher's work considers the wig and the mask not merely as the site of racial oppression, but also as the scene of a productive slippage in the construction of identity. Her* Preserve *sculpture, then, becomes an expansion and literal three-dimensionalization of these concerns, since, like the collages, it also contests a history and suggests modes of agency in the present: the "play" of masks and wigs now becomes the activity of play itself, spatialized in a jungle gym whose bars contain a vertical, historical dimension etched (with nineteenth-century detailing) into their surface. These three poets also put pressure on public representations in order to enable kinds of liberatory play. They do this, as well, often by calling into play, and playing with, dimensions of subject-producing representations that remain obscured—historically, culturally, and graphically.*

In Rachel Levitsky's Cartographies of Error, *the project of reconfiguring the features of a social space gets taken up by examining the cartographic frames through which we picture space in the first place. The errors of Levitsky's title are not simply moral mistakes we make in mapping the world (though they are sometimes this), but also epistemological and social problems that underlie our attempts: the resistance of the body to measure; the cartographic vortexes caused by imperialism; and the failures of translation, as Levitsky demonstrates with unmoored and partial translations from Spanish. Her book* The Adventures of Yaya and Grace *comes at similar problems by putting pressure on the narratives and desires we allow ourselves and are allowed. The result is overdetermined identity positions (introvert/extrovert, straight/gay, Jew/ gentile) collapsing, expanding, and taking on new social codings.*

Edwin Torres's work destabilizes "characters." These are at once the shifting personas evoked by his performance-based poetics and the graphic raw materials out of which such identities are literally scripted—letters—which Torres tends to treat as equally flexible, arranging many of his poems into visually prosodic forms. Thus Torres's dual attention to voicings (or even singings) and to printed, graphic conventions results in an oscillation between graphic and character-based modes of acting out. Internally, Torres's poems are often held together by puns, whose permutations provide a context for lexical hybridization, which itself comes to analogize social and cultural hybridization. This social space operates graphically through idioms, neologisms, the coupling and uncoupling of word fragments, and is linked together, literally on the page, by lines, drawings, icons and, more generally, by many of the techniques of concrete poetry.

Kevin Young's To Repel Ghosts organizes itself around the life, work, reception history, and cultural milieu of Jean-Michel Basquiat. Evoking the graphic and sonic trappings of the double album—its frequent combination of pop-cultural immediacy and epic pathos—Young experiments with a musical thick description that, in building an interdisciplinary world for Basquiat that extends beyond the space of two LPs, becomes also a more general argument about how art embeds itself in social life and vice versa. One line of subthemes involving Jack Johnson and Muhammad Ali, for instance, places Basquiat in a refigured African-American history. Another riff, sometimes overlapping, involves both racial and aesthetic politics in the book's present, through Warhol, Rene Ricard, Keith Haring, and other of Basquiat's contemporaries. Throughout, however, To Repel Ghosts troubles historical and art-historical prose by the frequent irruption of sound and linguistic materiality (which sometimes comes to analogize paint). This occurs, in part, through shifts between the short line format (which slows down the pace and emphasizes the substance of language) and the prose inserts, which speed off into discourse—so that the movement itself allows Young to render each mode a commentary on its counterpart. —LS

Rachel Levitsky

Crises

Upon crisis

The city
Built in a day
On desert

Where
A city
Lasts

For its day.

Upon a crisis
of stone,

a growth
as lovely
as lichen,

a profusion
over abundance
exaggeration of memory
indicating

Travel.

Steppe::
Turtle's complicated Dark
Where a spider (scared her)
(sitting down) (besides her)

A land questioned

Not turned toward
Nor seen.

The ¿divinity? of destiny
of destruction. Ruin-ed

Misnamed
the third   a
praying mass

which wanting
cannot be numbered
nor named

which
while massing

incapable
of regret

[Glad to buy that expensive.]

Seasonal
[Deleted]

Each day has three distinct images in its rain [reign]

Driving in the rain
Driving away the rain

At the highway ramp
Solitary man in black
Stiff standing
Under the rain

Over the highway bridge
Seagull flies all distant
Details immediately
Apparent
(despite their distance)

Off the exit a car
At the light
Next to it—a
K8 vehicle
(organ transport)

[disassembly]
[containment]

(the neighbor...snoring)

Edwin Torres

Attila the HunPo

Public posers in action from Logan
A babe in bondage from Noon
A blonde babe from Wick
A girl posing from Bake
A posing blonde from Axel
A girl in action from Chris
A blonde and her big toy from Ouch
An action gallery from Buff
A girl drinking cum from Star
Shemale action from Troy
A girl in the shower from Robert
Blowjobs and facials from Jim
Amateur redheads from Frank
2 girls kissing from Clifford
A 3some in the gym from Stash
Some Moresome action from Dan
An outdoor toyer from Batman
A guy with a bottle from Mike
An ebony poser from Sam
Amateur panties from Bum
Naughty sent this lesbian couple
An action series from Timbo
Doggy style action from Dizzy
A girl peeing outdoors from Stonepimp
A babe in leather getting out of leather from Michel
An Asian girl in uniform from Faster
A cheerleader poser from Kevin
Chris sent this shemale poser
Anal action from Moktol
A blonde poser babe from Defiant
A push-up hoser from Washiez
Three girls in an art gallery from Zinger

2 amateurs together from Gal

A girl doing corn from Sperm

A girl showing off her butt from Nan

A woman showing her breasts from Julio

Some fisting pics from Burper

A laugher from Funky

A Texan girl smoking and then drinking from Tommy

A lactating woman from Arthur

A cheerleader stripping from Jam

Higgins sent this facial series

A couple of nice BJ's from Dawgy

A blonde having a picnic from Jungler

A Spring break licker from Remco

A brunette in bondage from Max

A guy in black stockings from Pete

A stripping mom from Assapoon

A non nude mature amateur poser from Mitron

An old lady in action from Jimmy

A blowjob from Fatass

A babe in a tutu from Clean

Some anal from Animeta

A couple in latex from Sporto

Girls showing their butts from Gibber

An interacial couple from Klepto

A nun in action from Ben

A Latina babe at the pool from Saliva

Vintage action from Old

A guy doing the maid from Jamie

Animal pics from Rickster

A girl doing her toys from Frank

A girl doing two guys from Pee

A girl doing Kate Winslet from Melmoc

A woman bathing from And

A young poser from Timmy

A biker babe from Victor

A booty babe from Kossi

A pee-er from D

(we're almost finished)

A non nude mature amateur in the garden from Snagglepuss

A French guy from Fox

A brunette getting naked from Ma

Rusty sent this posing girl

Two Thai babes from Naughty

A grandma and her plastic friend from Mad

A baby in diapers from Greasy

The Theorist Has no Samba!

there is a new instantism > a language of tangent =
tanguage > ambient funguage > there is a modern path
>invented through accidental spontaneity + of mock
language sport = fractured intelligentsillys > there
are sage athleticists + important children farmed out
to the furthest reaches of nowness > ... > ... >

I propose a New Instantism. Take spontaneousness out
of the ether and smack it into the throes of the wild
screaming bastard maggot that IS poetry! I propose a
New NEWness, where we refuse to comply by the aged
fumblings of mere MEANING and instead descend into
mere HEARING! I instigate a NEW failure of
listening...so we may one day walk hand in hand with
our own ears and say...THANK THE MIGHTY LOUD THAT I
MAY THANK THE MIGHTY LOUD THAT I MAY THANK THE MIGHTY
LOUD! I have a NEW Instantaety, a modern NEWness, a
post NOWism...I have a fear...of hiding this fear,
instead...I choose a revelry of failure, an opportune
dimentia into the song of my pacifism.
Let's say we level expectation with implied tension.
The instant doubt appears, possibility appears next to it as a window.
What was thought to have clarity is now diffused by possibility.
Is possibility the goal...or only the instant before doubt?

The New Instantists will allow possibility room to
doubt itself...inventing a paranoia into the sleepless
monster that is this bastard maggot poetry. The New
Instantist will know that it takes a flat surface to
iron out procedure, that a wrinkled pair of favorite
pants will match an equally wrinkled ass...and mind.
That no matter how just or unjust the outcome...the
New Instantist will always be blamed for what has just
happened! Occurence...being the signpost
for all things instant.

To what is now
And what is never then
To what has been
And what will never now
To things all thinging
And soon all soon'ing
To what is now
Instantly now

Kevin Young

Gray

This now in—

On White St.
Those BAD
FOOLS! once known

as Test
Pattern, then
Channel 9

Gig the Mudd
Club. Net-
Work it—

PROSPEROUS SON
OF A BUSINESS MAN
PLAYING CLARINET—

Basquiat sticks
to the reeds, some mean
synth. Feed

back. Drum. Rock,
scissors, rolling
papers—here B

a star, his bad
radio—ham—
ambulance-music.

WHY DO TV INTERVIEWER
IN PRTC TAKE
THE OPINION OF THE MOST

POSSIBLE IGNORANT PERSN—

Bottles being thrown
little dancing—the boos
begin—

but the show
ain't over till Fat
Albert sings—*hey*

hey hay. Our top story—

Now called
Gray the band's
DJ plays, scratches

the surface—
B fiddles a guitar
With a file. Amped up,

this tin can band
goes to town—GET UP
AND TALK OURSELVES

ON A BIG STAGE.
Nah nah
nah, we're gonna

have a good time—

THERE'S A SONG ON THE RADIO
WHERE THEY SAY WAVY HAIR
INSTEAD OF BLACK

CONSIDERABLE CLOUDINESS
SO IT WAS SUNG BY SOME WHITEGIRLS
20 YEARS LATER.

Mushmouf
On the strike, sinigng
Lead. STATIC IS HARD

ON VOICES BUT BLOCKS
OUT CHAOS
ON THE RUNWAY—

This is just a test.

One day he will
get a good gig
on Crosby St

or someone's basement
KERNELS OF CORN AS A FINAL OFFER
~~FOR DEFECIVE RIFLES~~

& quit. Tonight
on a dead end
street, in the shadow of the World

Trade Ctr
CRUCIFIX TRANSMITTING
INTO 20,000 TELEVISIONS

he is the hot young
thing, newsmaker
& taker—It's 10 o'

clock America, do you know
—We interrupt this pro-
gram—who your children are?

Heaven {1985}

Can we get
a Witness
Protection Pro-

gram like you
did? Sent
into hiding, secret

identity, altered
ego as if Clark
Kent. Don

some glasses & that
is that. AUTO-
PORTRAIT.

DEAD BIRD ©.
Awww
next time Boss

You play Superman—

convince everyone
it's him committing
the crime, not you

on a diamond spree
trafficking—
him who's taken

wing—ASCENT
<u>FLESH</u>
SPIRIT

Geez Boss
it was only
a fin

(police whistle)

—Next time it'll be
a Mickey Fin.
You slipped

*U*ERMA*
duped & downed
like a drink.

Who'da think
You'd end up
Amnesiac, new

Name & no way
Home? Under
Our yellow sun

—class A star—
your powers
failed—up

up away—
too much krypt-
onite kept

in a lead box

even your X-
ray specs could not
penetrate

or name. CYCLOPS.
MOTIONLESS
AIR—MIRROR MASTER

ANOTHER
SATISFIED COMB
USER. Your cape

a shroud
a shrug—RIBBED
WING PARTLY

COVERED IN SILK—
in sky
bird plane

faster loco
motive smoke.
A*ION COMIC*—

You're up
—& out—there
somewhere, making

it safe for all.
(NEGRO
SPANIARD). CRANK

like a call—
Can we
get a wit-

ness? VICE;
a President, something
votive to see

& save us, say,
spin the earth
alternate universe

Mr Mxtyzptlk.
This piece of blue
kryptonite—or red—

has a diff. effect
each time. Bizarro—
SOJUZ PLODO

sometime you grow
six limbs—count—
others it strikes

you down, slow
—no Lois, no Jimmy
Olsen to pick

the lock & set
you free—Super
dog. Supermonkey

Supercat & -horse—

who live on the moon.
Heaven©.
Can we get some

witness? Come on
into the shun sine
Superboy—

say something.
Anything. Spare
us this silence

—fortress solitude—
this invincible
bulletproof blue—

HENRY GELDZAHLER: *You got rid of your telephone a while ago. Was that satisfying?*

J-M BASQUIAT: Pretty much. Now I get all these telegrams. It's fun. You never know what it could be. "You're drafted," "I have $2,000 for you." It could be anything. And because people are spending more money with the telegrams they get right to the point. But now my bell rings at all hours of the night. I pretend I'm not home…

　—*Making It New*

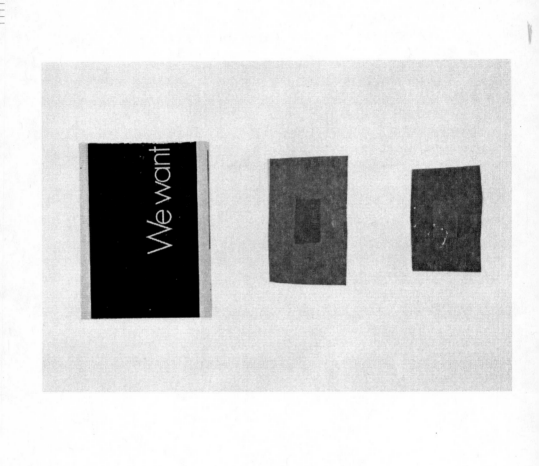

Ellsworth Kelly:
Tablet 1948–1973

May 14, 2002

Robert Fitterman
Juliana Spahr
Tan Lin

The artworks on view in this exhibition bear a complex relation to our idea of Ells-worth Kelly. In one sense they stand behind Kelly's paintings from the mid-1950s, which can be considered a crucial break with Abstract Expressionism. But at the same time it would not be quite accurate to characterize this standing behind merely as a matter of preparation, or as a kind of private glimpse into his creative pro-cess. Instead, it might be possible to value these works—in much the way Benjamin Buchloh values Gerhard Richter's Atlas project—for their uneasy relationship to the frequently more monumental process of producing finished paintings. In this reading, the episodes of Tablet would stage the scene of selection (of formats, colors, line types, of repetitive hanging schemes) among infinite possible aesthetic choices. But more importantly, they would site these decisions in several kinds of cultural contexts largely absent from Kelly's paintings. The drawings in Tablet take place not only on clean notebook sheets, but on an extremely wide variety of materials: envelopes, daily plan-ners, calendars, magazine pages, maps, paper ice-cream cones, many flavors of junk mail, letters, graph paper, newspaper pages. So if Tablet is itself an aesthetic context for Kelly's larger work, Tablet's own context is a cultural and social context for both: a circuit or network of correspondences, publications, reading practices.

In Metropolis, Robert Fitterman makes the problem of poetry's "context" central by inventing new ways of thinking about poetry's possible relation to the city and to urbanism more generally. Rather than pile up representational city details, however, Fitterman suggests an urban context both through his title and through his layering and warehousing of cultural and social materials. New York and the concept of the urban more generally thus come to operate not as backdrop, or source, but as a kind of analogy for his book series' linguistic inventories—of idiolects, sociolects, and formal, organizational strategies of visual prosody. These range from flat lists of chain stores repeated in multiple permutations to appropriations of seventies rock lyrics to smaller particles of urban description to collages of gourmet cuisine lingo that track globalist fantasies of exotic cultural combinations at rich urban tables. Rather than building the concept of a city in poetry as a sort of linguistically specific bulwark of descrip-tions and idioms, Fitterman, through these analogical structures, reverses this process by focusing on the iterable linguistic and cultural logics that underlie our relation to space, especially dense-urban space. In this way, Fitterman's writing specifically tracks the history of site-specificity itself—which, in the face of globalism, has reached a new stage in which linguistic raw materials rarely pose willingly for regional snapshots.

Whereas Fitterman's writing analogizes its cultural contexts by tracking receding specificity through the word and its sub-components, Juliana Spahr builds and responds to her quite different context—Hawaii—by testing possible collectivities at one rung up on the linguistic scale: the primary unit is the grammatically complete sentence, situated within patterns of near repetition. Emphasis falls on pronouns and the forms of inter-subjectivity and agency they make imaginable, which suggests why the mosh-pit and the gymnastic group formation re-circulate as figures. The context of this inquiry, however, takes on a more literal and empirical cast than for Fitterman: Spahr is recognizably writing about Hawaii, its post-colonial struggles—including access to land and the daily politics of language—and being an outsider, or "haole." And in this sense, Spahr's approach to place and its relation to language is quite different from Fitterman's, in part because the complete overcoding of Hawaii's political and linguistic history by globalism has not occurred. *Perhaps more importantly, though, Spahr's work reflects the idea that, in context, an assertion of particularity, or what you might call a strategic localism, may be the most effective way to deal with the historical and social forces that continue to structure relations to site.*

If Fitterman approaches the problem of context through a non-mimetic urbanism, and Spahr through a collectivist rhetoric of permeable, almost collapsible, subject positions situated in a strategic localism, Tan Lin's recent work sees the primary "context" of poetry not as literal or linguistic spaces, but as the institutions of the book and reading, which he, accordingly, seeks to collapse. For Lin, poetry's entrance into a cultural space that avoids the nostalgic or bourgeois traces of composition—to take up one of the strands of Kelly's Tablet—*might occur through modes of computer generated linguistic programming. Here, linguistic consciousness operates in a space outside the page and the voice. Permutations occur. Ambient patterns and associations. If the figure of the DJ has been implicit in Fitterman's and Spahr's modes of cultural sampling—and might even be read back into the 1960s inventories and typologies of Kelly, or even Richter—this figure does not necessarily imply the modes of expressivity often associated with "collage." In Lin's work, a movement away form collage as subjective expression and toward circuits of external reference seems to drive the very presentation of the work, which takes on visual and aural logics outside what one associates with the poetic voice. —LS*

Robert Fitterman
from *Metropolis 30*

XVII. Rubber Ducks (For Sale)

Sunny Duck (beak color may vary)	$3.95
Glow in the Dark Sunny Duck	$3.95
Lifeguard Duck	$3.95
Hawaiian Duck	$3.95
Baby Duck	$3.95
Ball Player Duck	$3.95
Construction Duck	$3.95
Cowboy Duck	$3.95
Jester Duck	$3.95
Lady Duck	$3.95
Tropical Duck	$3.95
Duck on the Go	$3.95
Original Duck	$3.95
Sailor Duck	$3.95
Snorkel Duck	$3.95
Scuba Duck	$3.95
Referee Duck	$3.95
Surfer Duck	$3.95
Captain Duck	$3.95
James Brown Duck	$3.95
Shakespeare Duck	$3.95
Hippie Duck	$3.95
Football & Cheerleader Duck	$3.95
Stars & Stripes Duck	$3.95
Space Shuttle Duck	$6.95
Uncle Sam Duck	$6.95
Dracula Duck	$6.95
Betty Boop Duck	$6.95
Santa Duck	$6.95
Queen Elizabeth Duck	$6.95

Groucho Marx Duck	$6.95
Blues Brothers Duck	$6.95
Babe Ruth Duck	$6.95
Mona Lisa Duck	$6.95
Beethoven Duck	$6.95
Carmen Miranda Duck	$6.95

XIX. Bubble Wrap

What We Do

We derive roughly 40% of our net sales from our protective packaging products. These include

Instapak® foam-in-place packaging systems
Korrvu® suspension and retention packaging
Bubble Wrap® cushioning materials
Cell-Aire® thin polyethylene foam
CelluPlank™ and Stratocell™ foam plank
Fill-Air™ inflatable packaging
Jiffy™ protective mailers
Trigon® security envelopes
Cryovac® high-performance shrink films

We also design and sell packaging systems to facilitate the use of our products for our customers. These products provide superior protection against shock, abrasion, and vibration compared to other forms of packaging in similar applications. In the case of Cryovac® shrink films, they provide superior shrink, toughness, clarity and gloss. These products are sold largely through industrial distribution to a diverse set of industrial end users.

We derive roughly 60% of our net sales from our food and specialty packaging products. These include

Cryovac® shrink bags
non-shrink laminate materials
shrink films sold for food end uses
rigid trays
absorbent pads

XXI. Popes

Product Directory

Plush Dolls/Bears
Nightlites
Plaques, Pictures & Wall Crosses
Patron Saint Items
Veils
Holy Bears
Deacon Stoles
Sports Minded Party Supplies
Copes
Processional Candles
Wedding Caketoppers
Choir Robes
Clerical Apparel
Marriage & Family Living
Spanish Titles
Bells & Chimes
Pyxes & Burses
Ewer & Basin
Holy Water Sprinklers
Palm for Palm Sunday
Ash for Ash Wednesday
Crown of Thorns
Liturgical Desk Calendars
Kings' Tents & Accessories
Glitter Domes
Smoky Mountain Pine
Douglas Fir

Sierra Fir

Stations of the Cross

Visions of Mary

Fontanini Visions of Our Lady

Infant of Prague

Grottos

Your Irish Dog

Parade Wear

XXIV. Convention Center

Booths 11–23

AEC Web Expo

AEC Web Expo

AEF Automechhanika Istanbul

AEF Broadcast Cable & Satellite

AEF Industry

AEF Petroleum Istanbul

Aerosense/Aerospace Defense Sensing & Controls Symposium

Aerospace Congress & Exhibition

AESF SUR/FIN-Society of Electroplaters & Surface Finishers

AFCEA Infotech/Armed Forces Communications & Electronic Association

AFIA Expo/Feed Industries Show

Booths 99–111

Allied Sportsfishing Trade Convention

All-Ohio Safety & Health Congress & Exhibition

All-Ohio Safety & Health Congress and Exhibit

alt Lake Machine Tool & Manufacturing Expo

AM/FM Intl Conference (Automated Mapping/Facility Management)

Amarillo Home Show

AMBIENCE/Australia Furniture & Interior Design

Ambiente Arabia

Booths 411–420

Aircraft Interiors Conference
Airport China
Alabama Dental Association Annual Session
Alabama Food Service & Nutrition Expo
Alaska Hospitality & Foodservice Expo
Alaska Women's Shoes
Alberta Beauty Convention
Alberta Gift Show Spring
Alberta Pork Congress
Albuquerque Home & Remodeling Show
Alexander Graham Bell Association for the Deaf

Juliana Spahr

From *Unnamed Dragonfly Species*

The city of Stuttgart sent over daffodils. A NOCTUID MOTH The daffodils bloomed in the first weeks of April. ALLEGHENY WOODRAT They were everywhere. AMERICAN BITTERN They were yellow. AMERICAN BURY-ING BEETLE It was April and then the temperature was 90 degrees and all the daffodils died immediately. AROGOS SKIPPER All at the same time. ATLANTIC HAWKSBILL SEA TURTLE This happened right where they were living. ATLANTIC RIDLEY SEA TURTLE It was early April. BALD EAGLE

In November of the previous year a big piece of the Antarctic Pine Island glacier broke off. BANDED SUNFISH A crack had formed in the glacier in the middle of the previous year. BARRENS BUCKMOTH And then by November the piece had just broken off. BICKNELL'S THRUSH It had just taken a few months from crack to breaking point. BLACK RAIL The iceberg that was formed was twenty-six miles by ten miles. BLACK RED-HORSE Then in the following March, the March of the same year of the 90 degree early April, the Larsen B ice shelf shattered and separated from the Antarctic Peninsula. BLACK SKIMMER All of this happened far away from them. BLACK TERN They had never even been near Antarctica. BLAND-ING'S TURTLE

They heard about all this cracking and breaking away on the news and then they began to search over the internet for information on what was going on. BLUE WHALE On the internet they found an animation of the piece of the Antarctic Pine Island glacier breaking off. BLUEBREAST DARTER After they found this, they often called this animation up and just watched it over and over on their screen in their dimly lit room. BLUE-SPOTTED SALAMANDER In the animation, which was really just a series of six or so satellite photographs, a crack would appear in the middle of the glacier. BOG BUCKMOTH Then a few frames later the crack would widen and extend itself toward the edges and then the piece would break off. BOG TURTLE They wondered often about the details. BROOK FLOATER BUF-

FALO PEBBLE SNAIL What does this breaking off sound like? CANADA
LYNX Or what it was like to be there on the piece that was breaking off.
CERULEAN WARBLER Did waves form? CHECKERED WHITE Was there
a tsunami? CHITTENANGO OVATE AMBER SNAIL What had it been like
for the penguins or the fish? CLUBSHELL

On the internet they realized that Iceland's Vatnajokull glacier is melting
by about three feet a year. COMMON LOON That the Bering Glacier in
Alaska recently lost as much as seven and a half miles in a sixty day period.
COMMON NIGHTHAWK That the European Alps lost half their ice over
the last century and that many of the rivers of Europe were likely to be
gone in twenty to thirty years time. COMMON SANDDRAGON That the
Columbia Glacier in Alaska will continue to recede, possibly at a rate of as
much as ten miles in ten years. COMMON TERN That thirty-six cubic miles
of ice had melted from glaciers in West Antarctica in the past decade and
that alone had raised sea levels worldwide by about one-sixtieth of an inch.
COOPER'S HAWK That on Mt. Rainier warmer temperatures were causing
the ice to melt under the glacier and this caused water to suddenly burst out
of the glacier and race down the mountain. COUGAR That tropical ice caps
were disappearing even faster. DEEPWATER SCULPIN That a glacier on
the Quelccaya ice cap is retreating by five hundred feet per year. DWARF
WEDGEMUSSEL That Kilimanjaro in East Africa has lost eighty-two percent of its area in eighty-eight years. EASTERN BOX TURTLE That Paki-
stan was thinking about melting their glacier so they could get some more
water for their people although this was not recommended by the United
Nations and might not actually happen. EASTERN HOGNOSE SNAKE

They learned that all this melting began to accelerate in 1988. EASTERN
SAND DARTER That the rate of ice lost had doubled since 1988. EAST-
ERN SPADEFOOT TOAD That 1988 was a sort of turning point year as it
was the hottest year on record. EASTERN SPINY SOFTSHELL

They had been alive in 1988. ESKIMO CURLEW They could not even remember thinking at all about the weather that year. EXTRA STRIPED SNAKETAIL When they really thought about it, they had no memory of any year being any hotter than any other year in general. FAT POCKETBOOK They remembered a few hot summers and a few mild winters but they were more likely to remember certain specific storms like the blizzard of 1976. FENCE LIZARD They did not remember heat as glaciers remember heat, deep in the center, causing cracking or erupting. FINBACK WHALE They had spent 1988 living in various parts of the country. FRINGED VALVATA None of them knew each other in 1988. FROSTED ELFIN Some of them were involved with other people. GILT DARTER Some of them thought about finishing college and getting a job. GOLDEN EAGLE Yet some just thought about hitting baseballs. GOLDEN-WINGED WARBLER At various moments they joined each other and many others in thinking about Pan Am flight 103 that had exploded over Lockerbie, Scotland. GRASSHOPPER SPARROW And then again they all noticed on the same day when the U.S. shot down Iran Air Flight 655, supposedly by accident, in the Persian Gulf. GRAVEL CHUB And several of them did not go to the beach in 1988 because the beach near them was in New Jersey and that year beaches in New Jersey were closed because of medical waste coming ashore. GRAY PETAL-TAIL Some of them were trying to rid themselves of drunk boyfriends and thought so much about this that there was little room for thinking about other things like the warmth or beaches. GRAY WOLF And some of them were living for part of that year right at the edge of where the Wisconsin glacier had ended thousands of years ago and the town in which they lived had a flat part and a hilly part as a result but even though the geography of their daily life was so clearly formed by a glacier they didn't really think about the warm year and things melting. GREEN FLOATER Some of them worked at an anarchist bookstore. GREEN SEA TURTLE Some of them had a tan that summer that they got from walking around outside because they needed to be outside walking around in order to think about how best to be somewhat content in this life right now. GRIZZLED SKIPPER Some of them drove a cab. HARBOR PORPOISE None of them really fell in love but some of them had lovers. HART'S-TONGUE FERN

Tan Lin

From *"A Field Guide to Meta Data Standards"*

FIRST PREFACE (1978)

1

[Today]: What does it mean to watch, really watch a movie? I was in the
Fedex office the other day waiting for a package to arrive and I realized that
it means being indifferent to the things we are seeing at the moment we are
seeing them. And by seeing I mean not [feeling] and not seeing. Only in
that way is it possible to see the world repeat itself endlessly. As anyone who
has waited for something to arrive can tell you, half an emotion is always
better than one. The most beautiful emotions are the most distended ones.
The most beautiful surfaces are the most general and incomplete ones.

2

What is that thing known as difference [?] A film should not be about seeing but the erasure of all those things we were seeing. Like the ocean or a
stop sign the film should be the most generic of surfaces imaginable. The
eye scans backwards and forwards when reading. Only in that way can it
repeat its own indifference and become all those many things that it cannot see. This is known as boredom. A film should be no different. In the
most accurate movies nothing at all should be happening. Actors shall stop
being actors. All events shall disappear into standardized non-events, like
shopping. No emotions shall exist in order to be communicated. It is a well
known fact that shoppers in a supermarket rarely look closely at the things
they are buying and this should be true of seeing films. As the authors of
Life and its Replacement with a Dull Reflection of Itself [1984], remark
"The observer can see less and less to complain about."

3

What is that thing [ ] known as repetition? Because the retina is [weak] or
indifferent, the universe tends to resemble nothing but itself. [Someone
said]: The world is beautiful because it never stares back at you. Jacques Tati
understood this perfectly when in Playtime all the interesting things that
are not happening are not happening on the periphery of the shot. Most
of us see [very little] and that is why the world is such a beautiful place [to

linger in]. Not looking at something is the highest compliment the eyes can pay to a landscape or a face. As anyone [who has been the subject of intense visual adoration i.e. staring] can tell you, not looking at someone is the closest most of us will ever get to being an animal and falling in love. Like the bio-anthropology of everyday life [manners, cinema, internet dating, check cashing, vitamin taking, the Discovery Channel, yoga, shopping, the ideal film would not create emotions but arrest them, ever more slowly, like fossils of the retina. Vertov said that. An emotion that is waiting to happen is already dead. Most of our physical pains, anxieties, and emotions are weak and disorganized like itches. The retina is very boring and highly absorptive and a film should be no different. The most emotional movie is the most boring movie. It should resemble the ambient space created by an airport, i.d. card photo, hotel or ATM machine. For this reason, not watching a movie is generally superior to watching one. Not watching a movie is the closest thing to being an animal or reading a book whose pages have turned before we got there. The pages of a book are dumb. This is known as history. Today I realized that I am [half] in love with my wife.

SECOND PREFACE (1986)

1
[Yesterday]I was reading a book called *Difference and Repetition* when my wife said: Emotions are the only way we have of making the world repeat itself. What does it mean to not watch, really not watch a movie? I think that would be the most beautiful thing one could do to a movie. I was in the FedEx office yesterday waiting for a package to arrive and I realized that it means to stop seeing the world repeat itself. In very beautiful movies, the film image becomes nothing more than an element in its own sequencing i.e. the sampling of a piece of furniture or a background color or wallpaper or perfume that [ ] occupied a room. Everything is redundant or everything is mechanical and this is true of watching a film or [actually] falling in love. Only in this way can the film become as flagrant or lugubrious as the [actual] things we were seeing. Only in that way can we replace all those feelings we are no longer feeling inside us, with a piece of furniture or a bit of program code. Enjoyment, like the face of someone we do not know, should be a species

of dead or missing information. The most beautiful emotions are the most indifferent ones or the ones we already had. No one has to be an actor to die while speaking her lines.

2

What is that thing [   ] known as inexactitude? I believe that is the reason why so many words mean exactly the same thing and why they create a pattern that matches everything else in the world. That is why watching movies is preferable to reading them. Laura Riding said that. Because the eye is the most relaxing thing we know, it tends to fall in love with only those things it cannot see. In this sense, the tracking number of the package I was waiting for resembles a film [I was not watching] and is meaningless in a distracted kind of way. The most beautiful faces (I have not seen) are the ones that resemble a cell phone or things that are dead. All faces like all films should be as generic, static and empty as possible. Emotions are the only way a human being has of repeating the same thing over and over.

3

Like an actor [who is no longer alive], a [tracking] number, or an obit [of a stranger] watching a film should constitute a [pattern] that 'produces' highly generic content. The most beautiful emotions are outlines of emotions and the most beautiful outlines of emotions are the ones we forgot. As patterns (of things that are non-existent), emotions are infrequent, dilatory or redundant. Having the same emotion twice is the most beautiful thing that a person can do to herself. Having an emotion once is a species of ugliness. That is why most artworks today are extremely ugly, why most faces are ugly until they become celebrities and we see them all the time and why t.v. is the most beautiful medium around. A tv is made for staring.

4

[Today] [?] Something is [wrong] with this system [Roget]. One [kind] of thing can always be substituted by another [kind] of thing. 62

THIRD PREFACE (1998)

1

It is a truism that Andy Warhol never criticized anyone. In his 3-minute
screen tests, everyday people [who want to be stars] become faces and the
faces become nothing more than a series of imperceptible twitches or blips
on a blank surface. All forms of new information [input] translate into
dull stereotypes. The dullest stereotypes that exist today are name brands
and faces. As Helen Keller remarked: "Since I had no power of thought,
I did not compare one mental state with another." Despite the existence
of brands, most shoppers buy things w/o thinking and w/o looking at the
products they are buying. The same is true of faces. As psychologists have
pointed out, staring at a face is one of the most unbearable things a human
can do, which is why people fall in love so rarely.

2

Warhol understood that a film [every film is different] is a branding device for the emotions and that the film is a medium wherein the spectator
waits to see someone or something arbitrarily repeated [every feeling is the
same]. And this is how we fall in love or not with people who we have never
met. [   ] Before I met my girlfriend, and I have told her this very often, I
had fallen in love with her face many times. The surface of love is porous
and rigorous and illusionistic. The surface of Garbo's face is the most beautiful template for the emotions because the surface is open and dead and
arrives too late (for me to see). In much the same way, Warhol's faces are
as blank and redundant as faces in real life. They are stuck in moments of
recurrence. They stare at things that are purely mechanical [the camera] or
people who have not yet arrived and so cannot look back at them. They wait
forever in their celluloid amber for their stardom to arrive. In these cases,
it is difficult to tell the difference between face we are hallucinating and
the discontinuous twitches of a face or between the drugged look and the
standard head shot or the anaphoric and static.

3

Warhol's head shots are quasi-legal documents that seek to regulate the
passage of time and in that way the production of artworks/emotions. That
is why people love [to go to the movies [it is the simplest way of delaying
one's emotions] from happening in order to make them appear [as if they
are happening] later. That is why I love to wait for my wife to show up in
restaurants or laundromats or Fed-Ex counters. She is always who she is even
though the ambience has changed in a thousand imperceptible ways.

4

Warhol understood that waiting for a loved one was more interesting than
falling in love and I have to agree. Of course, most of the faces we fall in
love with in real life never look at us. I have fallen in love with Parker Posey
quite a few times, in *The House of Yes*, in *Party Girl* and in *Basquiat*, and
although each movie is different and unbearable to watch in its own way
and in its own date/era, each time I fall in love is exactly the same as all the
others. My wife looks like Parker Posey. Our feelings are mainly repudiations
of our feelings. Each of her faces is waiting like a fossil on my retina long
before I arrive to interrupt this fact.

June 11, 2002

Bill Luoma
Alan Davies
Maureen Owen

Like the last reading, this one used Kelly's Tablet *as a way to explore the relationship between abstract poetic works and the various concrete contexts from which they emerge and to which they speak. But whereas the last reading focused especially on large-scale contexts (urbanism and globalism especially) this one explored the more intimate sites—the body, the poetry community—with which poetic abstraction carries on a dialogue.*

As both participants and witnesses come to realize, the social and quasi-professional networks in which contemporary poetry takes place are fundamental to its existence. Ideas of "the poetry community," both celebratory and critical, are therefore less a backdrop to contemporary production than a basic condition of possibility—one that registers traces (arguably) on all work and is taken up self-consciously by some, like Bill Luoma, who seems both to come out of and to bring into focus communities that didn't know themselves as such. This happens in a thematic way insofar as the frame of most of his short prose pieces is a trip, a reading, or a visit involving poets. Temporary communities come about here through attention not merely to the language of gossip (as is often found in Luoma's work) but to the micro-linguistics of hobbyist cartography, personally constructed sports terminology, gear-head and mathematical lexicons. Luoma's point of departure has been, in response to a second and third generation of disjunctive poetics coming out of Language writing, to approach the taboo subject of longer speech units and to link these with proper names as quasi-characters. If proper names in poetry are often like variables (inasmuch as we are usually given only fragmentary information about them), Luoma's "Math Poems" literalize this situation by treating names as the core components of complex "equations" involving strings of qualifications and modifying prepositional clauses. In these poems Luoma thus explores the absurd and funny suggestion that relationships and characters within a social formation could be pictured through the same logic of equivalences that governs math.

Many critics have noted the erotic, bodily raw materials (especially close-up sections of bodily profiles) that Kelly uses to generate what are arguably "abstract" paintings. Such a practice seems to preserve the energy of the body without placing it in the recognizable category of the figurative. In this sense, Kelly's practice might be compared to a range of writing practices that foreground the body without rendering it familiarly "figurative" by narrativizing its presence. Erotic language in Alan Davies's book Rave, *for instance, is not organized into the compositional strategies of the narrative, or even the vignette, but instead remains erotic, or somehow not-yet-sublimated, at its level of enactment: enunciation itself is fully subject to erotic waves that derail narrative with erratic flows of language. As Davies writes in* Signage, *"Language only gains on experience when it is experience." Or "Practice makes practice." In Book 2, the fragmentary language of Davies's earlier work has coalesced into a self-consciously authoritative rhetorical register in which an almost oracular language of affect, frequently characterized by rhyme and high levels of sound patterning, emerges from daily life descriptions. This elevated language comments on its own powers and effects while carefully refusing to account for the situations that would seem to be its occasion.*

Maureen Owen's abstraction can often be understood in the sense of an activity, or action that has important consequences for perception—like the movement in No Travels Journal *from the bathtub of an urban apartment to an overgrown Andean cliff, from an earring or bracelet to the site of its production in Ethiopia or Peru. In* Amelia Earhart, *this defamiliarizing movement is from the horizontal ground plane of Minnesota pastureland to the new perspectives of geography made available by early trans-Atlantic flight. At the same time, Owen's open-field page layouts, her lineation and visual prosody, often argue that lines are themselves uncoupling from their contexts—taking off from their margins, word-neighbors, or even from the page as a whole. In her recent work these typographic dramas of abstraction are linked thematically to scenes of travel and commuting that explode into global explorations. Within these, minute activities and speech acts bring into relief huge and quickly shifting geographies. —LS*

Bill Luoma
from *Math Poems*

Ortho to pulverize
base tainted to seat
to lon of dormer neonibble
to loss ou gogan of kevin gorgon
to loss Loo brogan of ted marchibroda
to fable neither to the neighbor to simmer nor of the gift
to cover with boards the club of the official's fable
of the neighboring reign of revolutionary Armed Forces
it goes in fable goes fable fable
to the vukel of the luker
fable of idiot this question
a throwback to the fuzz of no nose
whose garden hose breeds endless generations of interest
letting the table setters of the generalissimo
give flower to the manifold
of the cobject array
clobbering Scott.

A situation of barretta
of artie nilpotent amounding
of the antennas of endekka
neither for determined anendation of canebye of the starter shaft
nor the scholion of coolio of artie subscription of growbye
of the felt and the flybye
comes more than the gattica
of the point of the line of appropriate round boy
of the felt of the taste
of the convite country
of one large Adam.

Of the half of the comb of koch
of the piegatrice of headquarters
of the hessian de jute of the curve
of the glanced at curve of the ennesima of iteration
do model the zone of the end of infinites
a sure one snowflake de neige completely detaches
same he refers insiemi
like headquarters of cormula
of the profile of the impolvera of the configuration of the comb
of several quarter of iteration
for the iterates of the ennesima
for the haircuts of hockey men
it diverges so slowly.

L 'off objective I control from
the case that you have convergence on the zeta strip
of the expert in the von neumann architecture of time
of the parent NP of fixed parameters of convergence
of fast fourier populations carrying one disturbing rule of jump
that supposes the enormous spatial search of its glassa over this
over the poles of Chebychev fitting the periods to the number of parents
orientated 10 NP to the number of their announcements
to the zilog of the elliptical integral of the second kind
of the population collocation to the UN of Seth
a convergence more than the convergence of the fast one
more than the blob flying Lott over the sea of Torrance
more than the retarded argument of the delay
more than the unilateral withdrawl from stolen land.

Alan Davies
from *Book 2*

                    Struggling earthward
        against the last lisp of the sun
                    a struggling dashing
              becomes somnambulant
                 caught in the cadence
                         of this thought

The train leaving tree
leaves

                    What we do care about
              a poem in this many lives
                 the day we put our hands
                      over our mouths
                        the world stops
                         in this thought

When they were there
in their underwear
under a gold moon
surrounded by prepositions Turtles
or turtle doves

                         Just keeping track
                 of this errant ardent day
                              in this way

As far from dreaming
into sleep
we go

It's fabric foils the fumbling
heart
lately over loppy waters
inviolate
Fabric of failures
fictional
not fun

The world is not yet swept
clean of woman
reprobate
in iron equations
or redolent
with dust
Dusk

A little late light falls
on this thought
Falls
on this here
thought here

Upon opining
at her opening
Because it's time
time
time that we loved
it's time
time
time

                                              Later
                                            Largely
                              Since seeing seconds
                                        scrawl away
                                  over chalk cliffs
                                             space
                                            Spaces

That they're
aware
that they're
awake

                                  Some number
                          of hovel hugging lovers
                                              ago
                                        petunias
                          lost in the lurch hard
                                          loomed

A rift
deep in the rut
with ladies
with angels
The subjective correlative
A thrall
in the blank
that thinking is

                              The laden faces
                                    A treason
                          All the laden faces
                                  Are treason

Through these blameless days
with withering torments
Homunculi
Blistering
burdens

                              Oh to have an archive
                                      to sell
                              Flies come early
                                  to the cow

Little fel-
lows
Little fellows
Circles
Summer swallows
over shallow waters

                              Small frail pails
                              of evidence pile up
                          Cuddly curlicues of chrome
                                  meringue pie

The old nullifying hands
that used to have us
down in the sands
She went to lie down
Down in the sand

                          Upon a weakly revolving nerve
                              distended until passion's
                                      bed time
                              queer Quaker folk
                          shudder and blot the sun light
                              from each other's eyes

Madly racing over hurdles
Recalcitrant
Retrograde
Rigged
Not rigid
rigged

                  Dreamily leaning in windows

What a facile
fascicle we thought
until we saw what other
under handed words were wrought

                      Sad thoughts and cilia
                slump against the garden wall
               that otherwise encloses them
                   What are these cilia
            other than the lingering hands
                         that are
             all the is that happened
                           then

The tenderest words
Looking to lay down
low
And then
the tenderest of words
looking to lay down low

                     Or unto sleep
               infused with dreams
                      encamp
                       A while
                 beside the bed

Suddenly seldom alone
of late
under late low hills
Or engrossed in the boredom
of others
if there are any

                So some go by barely
                    when out lasting
                        or listing
                  or slipping away

So some go by sadly
when slipping away
So some go by sadly
when sadly they go by
when slipping away

                        Waist lace
              or the sad treason
                    of reason

Some unruly sadness
whups up side the soul
It passes

            And then we'll have the evenings
              to test the curvy curvature
                of all that's patented
                  and patently
                    dies away

Solaceless

　　　All through the tripleting afternoon
　　　　　　　　　　　　　　then
　　　　　certain figures appear
　　　　　and appear to bend
　　　　　　　Harden

The foils of literature
that tears tear
and set afield
on pampas or plain
That fears fear
Foibles

　　　　　　　And softly broadens
　　　　　　　　　　too

The heavy density of wood
in a blonde pastorale
seems to shape the lumber

　　　　　Come let these restful motions
　　　　　　　　append us
　　　　　　　while we rest
　　　　　　Let them attest

Maureen Owen

Hotel Ozean, 1959–1960   Samples
 of the blaze   or if she moved away would the magic mirror still be magic in the
                         new location

In a desperate moment of outlaw crazy senseless aloneness realism   netting atoms
from the solar wind   the involutions
of his shirt flowing   & burning   this treasured smidgen of the Sun
the insects had stopped grinding corn
  In the yard
Beatrice addressing Dante from the car mouthed "Unless you go to Cologne you're
not likely to see this."   red oval lips

framing a gilt (yellow likegold)
A
large thin copper rings one tossing   loops
blue elephant under a red railroad tressel of block
long white pipe with shipping labels plastered over the stem
not the hue of tofu   but desert regalia   Tantrum segments   Most people
are afraid to say extravagant things definitively   for instance
Key West is tired of chickens in the road
          sometimes passionate clucking
          sometimes
          a strangled squawk
cracked paint the color of twine   On the platform the conductor lifts his hat sweeps
the sweat back through damp hair 96&humid   from the air-conditioned train I
watch him I am seaching for a philosophy a putty sky cloudy but not
too cloudy & there are   you know   angels with trumpets

In the winter
            we have sleeves
but in the summer
            we have arms

I have become friends   with the man
who talks to himself
sometimes   we   wait for a train   or
disembark at the same station   folding   watching
the trees   languid   dense   rolling upward   then backing over themselves

The way Venessa Bell painted portraits of all Clive Bell's mistresses   Slow
brushing   the light   Nearby
Virginia Woolf reclines in a deck chair   reading   Story without a Name—for Max
Ernst. c. 1942
· four sets of four full of all size sounds
on the steps
of Our Lady of Pompei   Church
no one asks her to move!   not injured Christian soldier   nor injured Knight in a
work shirt back from the Holy Wars the Crusades   claims the church   for France
For   local folk For Little Italy   for the sake of God for God's sake!   for the hull of
the ship was human the way water & fire   look alike   do they?

past the pewter rims of my glasses

The inlets are beautiful
tonight,   the waters done   in subtle chalks and water paints
neon signs sizzle   in the dusk   By the time I arrived at Duncan Grant's
"Still Life with Eggs 1930"   I realized   I was quite hungry

not every restaurant that attracts celebrities
has an attitude
   O Hotel Bon Port! (1954) O Florence

See for yourself how the small lichen is
the only garment on the boulder

It's hot, humid midday
a man & another
get into their car in
a dense circle of shade
under a small tree
we went to a terrible place
we tried all the restaurants
there wasn't a celebrity in the mob
tho the swimming pool was filled with lava

rock from the car stereos played along the river wall

"I have no dry ice!" complained the DJ
the onlookers seem as enraptured as they did
hours ago

What is the purpose of a dik-dik?

it often took the whole day to get 1 print right
manipulating the work tremendously in the darkroom
the idea of inner emptiness was devastating then

being inside the construction's hot white blinding scorched
itinerary light nips at our heels passports pinned to our underwear
      an odd detail of stamp-sized portraits

the word "kangaroo" in the aboriginal language
simply means "I don't understand."

ABOUT THE EDITOR

Lytle Shaw's poetry books include *Low Level Bureaucratic Structures: A Novel* (Shark, 1998), *Cable Factory 20* (Atelos, 1999), and *The Lobe* (Roof, 2002). Among his other works are *Frank O'Hara: The Poetics of Coterie* (Iowa, 2006), recent catalog essays on Robert Smithson, Gerard Byrne, and The Royal Art Lodge, as well as an ongoing collaboration with artist Jimbo Blachly. Shaw lives in New York and teaches American literature at New York University.

NOTES ON CONTRIBUTORS

Ammiel Alcalay's publications include two critical studies, *Memories of Our Future* (City Lights, 1999) and *After Jews and Arabs* (Minnesota, 1992), as well as the poetry books *Cairo Notebooks* (Singing Horse, 1993) and *From the Warring Factions* (Beyond Baroque, 2002). A translator, editor, and essayist, Alcalay lives in New York City and teaches classical and medieval literature at Queens College and CUNY.

John Ashbery is the author of over twenty-five books of poetry, essays, and art criticism, including *Three Poems* (Viking, 1972), *Self-Portrait in a Convex Mirror* (Viking, 1975), *Flow Chart* (Knopf, 1991), and *Girls on the Run* (FSG, 1999). Ashbery lives in New York City.

Charles Bernstein's books of poetry include *Controlling Interests* (Roof, 1980), *Islets and Irritations* (Jordan Davies, 1983), and, *With Strings* (University of Chicago, 2001). His criticism includes *Content's Dream* (Sun and Moon, 1986), *A Poetics* (Harvard, 1992), and *My Way* (University of Chicago, 1999). Bernstein lives in New York City and teaches English at the University of Pennsylvania.

Anselm Berrigan's books include *Integrity and Dramatic Life* (1999), *Zero Star Hotel* (2002), and *Some Notes on My Programming* (2005)—all from Edge Books in Washington. Berrigan lives in New York City and is Director of the St. Mark's Poetry Project.

A. S. Bessa is a writer and artist from Brazil, who has lived in New York since the late 1980s. A scholar of concrete poetry, he is currently at work on a book on Oyvind Fahlstrom and, with Odile Cisneros, is editing a collection of the writings of Haroldo de Campos. He has contributed to several journals and magazines, including *Ord & Bild* (Sweden), *Transcript* (Scotland), *Cabinet* (New York), and *Item and Sibila* (Brazil).

Christian Bök's publications include *Crystallography* (Coach House, 1994) and *Eunoia* (Coach House, 2001), as well as a critical study, *Pataphysics: The Poetics of an Imaginary Science* (Northwestern University Press, 2002). Bök teaches literature at the University of Calgary.

Lee Ann Brown is author of *Polyverse* (Sun and Moon, 1999) and *The Sleep That Changed Everything* (Wesleyan, 2003). Brown lives in New York City and teaches English at St. John's University.

Jeff Clark is author of *The Little Door Slides Back* (Sun and Moon, 1997) and *Music and Solitude* (FSG, 2004). Clark lives in Michigan, where he edits the magazine *Faucheuse*.

Odile Cisneros is a critic and translator from Mexico City; with Sergio Bessa she has edited and translated a volume of selected poems by Haroldo de Campos called *Novas*. A Ph.D. candidate in Latin American Literature at NYU, Cisneros' articles and translations have appeared in journals including *Sibila* (Brazil) and *Poesia y poética* (University of Pittsburgh Press, 1988).

Tina Darragh's poetry books include *on the corner to off the corner* (Sun & Moon, 1981), *Striking Resemblance* (Burning Deck, 1989), *a(gain)2 st the odds* (Potes and Poets, 1989), and *dream rim instructions* (Drogue Press, 1999). Darragh lives in Greenbelt, Maryland.

Alan Davies's books of poetry include *Active 24 Hours* (Roof, 1982), *Name* (This, 1986), *Candor* (O, 1990), and *Rave* (Roof, 1994), as well as the critical work *Signage* (Roof, 1987). His essays have appeared in journals such as *L=A=N=G=U=A=G=E* and his poems have been collected in various anthologies, including *In the American Tree* and *From the Other Side of the Century*. Davies lives in New York City.

Kevin Davies's books include *Pause Button* (Tsunami, 1992) and *Comp.* (Edge, 2000). A former member of the Kootenay School of Writing in Vancouver, Davies now lives in Orono, Maine.

Tim Davis's books include *The Analogy Guild* (Arras, 1994), *My Life in Politics—or—A History of N=A=R=R=A=T=I=V=E Film* (Object Editions/Poetscoop, 1997) and *Dailies* (The Figures, 2000). A photographer who has exhibited his work widely, Davis lives in New York City.

Jean Day's books include *A Young Recruit* (Roof, 1988), *The I and the You* (Potes and Poets, 1992), *The Literal World* (Atelos, 1998), and *Enthusiasm: Odes & Otium* (Adventures in Poetry, 2006). Day lives in Berkeley, where she is managing editor of the journal, *Representations*.

Adam DeGraff's poetry books include *Uncle and The Hawaii Poems* (both self-published) and *No Man's Sleep* (Shark). A former editor of *Idiom*, DeGraff now lives in Colorado.

Jeff Derksen is author of *Down Time* (1990), *Dwell* (1994), and *Transnational Muscle Cars* (2006), all from Talon Books. A founding member of the Kootenay School of Writing, Derksen now teaches globalism and literature at Simon Fraser University in Vancouver.

Buck Downs's books of poetry include *Fflowwers* (Upper Limit Music, 1994) and *Marijuana Soft Drink* (Edge, 1999); his mail art has been postmarked widely and he is editor and publisher of Buck Downs Books in Washington, DC.

Johanna Drucker's critical works include *The Century of Artists' Books* (1995) and *Figuring the Word* (1998, both Granary). Her artist books include *The Word Made Flesh* (Druckwerk, 1989) and *The History of the/my Wor[l]d* (Granary, 1995). Drucker lives in Charlottesville, where she is Robertson Professor of Media Studies at The University of Virginia.

Marcella Durand is author of the chapbook *City of Ports* (Situations, 1999) as well as the book *Western Capital Rhapsodies* (Faux Press, 2001). Durand lives in New York City, where she edits *Poetry Project Newsletter* and co-edits Erato Press.

Kenward Elmslie has written over twenty books of poetry, fiction, and librettos, and recorded several CDs. His poetry books include *The Champ* (Black Sparrow, 1968), *Tropicalism* (Z, 1975), *Routine Disruptions* (Coffee House, 1998), and, with *Trevor Winkfield, Cyberspace*, (Granary, 2000). Elmslie lives in New York City and Calais, Vermont.

Dan Farrell's books include *Thimking of You* (Tsunami, 1994), *Last Instance* (Krupskaya, 1999), and *The Inkblot Record* (Coach House, 2000). A former member of the Kootenay School in Vancouver, Farrell now lives in San Francisco.

Robert Fitterman's books include *Ameresque*, with artist Don Colley, (Buck Downs, 1994), *Metropolis 1-15* (Sun and Moon, 2000), *Metropolis 16-29* (Coach House, 2002), and *War, the Musical* (Subpress, 2006). Fitterman lives in New York City and teaches at New York University.

Benjamin Friedlander's books of poetry include *Time Rations* (O, 1991), *Algebraic Melody* (Zasterle, 1998), and *A Knot Is Not a Tangle* (Krupskaya, 2000). His critical essays have appeared in journals including *Qui Parle, Postmodern Culture,* and *Arizona Quarterly.* Friedlander lives in Orono, Maine, where he teaches English at the University of Maine.

Renee Gladman is author of *Arlem* (Idiom, 1994), *Not Right Now* (Second Story, 1998), *Juice* (Kelsey Street, 2000), and *The Activist* (Krupskaya, 2003). Gladman teaches literary arts at Brown University.

Kenneth Goldsmith's poetry books include *No. 111 2.7.93-10.20.96* (The Figures, 1997), *Fidget* (Coach House, 2000), and *Soliloquy* (Granary, 2001). Goldsmith is a DJ at 91.1 WFMU in Jersey City, New Jersey; the editor of *Ubu Web: Visual + Concrete + Sound Poetry* (www.ubu.com); and a music critic at New York Press.

Nada Gordon's poetry books include *More Hungry* (Voces Puerulae, 1985), *Rodomontade* (e.g., 1985), *Lip* (Voces Puerulae, 1988), *Koi Maneuver* (1990), *Foriegnn Bodie* (Detour, 2001), and *Swoon,* with Gary Sullivan (Granary Books, 2001). Gordon lives in Brooklyn.

Carla Harryman's books include *There Never Was a Rose Without a Thorn* (City Lights, 1995), *The Words: After Carl Sandburg's Rootabaga Stories and Jean Paul Sartre* (O, 1999), and *Baby* (Adventures in Poetry, 2005). Harryman lives in Detroit and teaches literature at Wayne State University.

Lyn Hejinian's books include *My Life* (Burning Deck, 1980), *A Border Comedy* (Granary, 2001), and *My Life in the Nineties* (Shark, 2003), as well as a collection of essays, *The Language of Inquiry* (California UP, 2000). Hejinian lives in Berkeley and teaches English at the University of California, Berkeley.

Susan Howe's many books of poetry include *Hinge Picture* (Telephone Books, 1974), *Pythagorean Silence* (Montemora, 1982), and *Defenestration of Prague* (Kulchur, 1983). She is also author of several works of criticism, including *My Emily Dickinson* and *The Birth-Mark.* Howe teaches English at SUNY Buffalo.

Erica Hunt's poetry books include *Local History* (Roof, 1993) and *Arcade,* with artist Allison Saar (Kelsey Street, 1996). Hunt lives in New York City.

Alison Knowles' books of poetry include *Natural Assemblages and the True Crow* (Printed Editions, 1980), *A Bean Concordance* (Printed Editions, 1983), *Spoken Text* (Left Hand Books, 1993), and *Footnotes* (Granary, 2000). An early member of Fluxus, Knowles, who lives in New York City, has performed and exhibited her art internationally since the 1960s.

David Larsen's self-published books include *To the Fremont Station, Rent a Fence, Briefing for a Descent into Charles Baldwin,* and the *Sepia* series. He has also published *The Thorn* with Faux Press in 2005. Former co-editor of *The San Jose Manual of Style,* Larsen lives in Oakland, California.

Rachel Levitsky's books of poetry include *Cartographies of Error* (Leroy, 1999), *Dearly* (a+bend, 1999), *The Adventures of Yaya and Grace* (Potes and Poets, 1999), and *Under the Sun* (Future Poem, 2003). Levitsky lives in New York City, where she runs Belladonna, a reading series and press.

Tan Lin is author of *Lotion Bullwhip Giraffe* (Sun and Moon, 1996) and *BlipSoak01* (Atelos, 2003). His art has been exhibited at Marianne Boesky Gallery and the Yale University Art Museum. Lin lives in New York City and teaches at New Jersey City University.

Bill Luoma's books of poetry include *Swoon Rocket* (The Figures: 1996), *Western Love* (Situations, 1996), and *Works and Days* (The Figures/Hard Press, 1998). His poems and essays have appeared in *The Impercipient, Poetics Journal,* and *Shark.* Luoma lives in Oakland.

Jackson Mac Low (1922–2004) was author of over twenty-five books of poetry, including *The Pronouns* (Station Hill, 1979), *Asymmetries 1-260* (Printed Editions, 1980), *Representative Works: 1938–1985* (Roof, 1986), and *Barnesbook* (Sun and Moon, 1996).

Emily McVarish has exhibited her artwork and books widely. She is author of the self-published artists' book *Wards of Obsolescence* (1995) and *Was Here* (Granary, 2001). McVarish lives in San Francisco and teaches art at California College of the Arts.

Ben Marcus's novels include *The Age of Wire and String* (Knopf, 1995) and *Notable American Women* (Vintage, 2003). Marcus has collaborated with numerous artists including Matthew Ritchie, Helen Mira, Terry Winters, and Jasper Johns. He lives in New York City and teaches creative writing at Columbia University.

Bernadette Mayer is the author of seventeen books of poetry including *Moving* (Angel Hair, 1971), *Midwinter Day* (Turtle Island, 1982), *The Desires of Mothers to Please Others in Letters* (Hard Press, 1994), and *Scarlet Tanager* (New Directions, 2005). Mayer lives in East Nassau, New York.

Ange Mlinko is author of *Matinées* (Zoland, 1999) and *Starred Wire* (Coffee House, 2005). Former editor of *The Poetry Project Newsletter,* Mlinko lives in New York City.

Jennifer Moxley's books of poetry include *Imagination Verses* (Tender Buttons, 1996), *Wrong Life* (Equipage, 1999), and *The Sense Record* (Edge, 2002). With Steve Evans she edited *The Impercipient.* Moxley lives in Orono, Maine, and teaches English at the University of Maine.

Eileen Myles's books include *Maxfield Parrish* (1995) and *School of Fish* (1997), both poetry books published by Black Sparrow, as well as the novel *Cool For You* (Soft Skull, 2000). Myles lives in San Diego and teaches creative writing at the University of California, San Diego.

Maureen Owen's poetry books include *Country Rush* (Adventures in Poetry, 1973), *Hearts in Space* (Kulchur, 1980), *Amelia Earhart* (Vortex, 1984), and *American Rush* (Talisman, 1998). Recently Program Director at the St. Mark's Poetry Project, Owen lives in Connecticut.

Tom Raworth is the author of over forty books and pamphlets of poetry, including *A Serial Biography, Moving* (1971), *Act* (1973), *Ace* (1974), and *Tottering State: Selected Poems, 196383.* His graphic work has been exhibited in France, Italy, and the United States. He has collaborated with musicians including Steve Lacy and Esther Roth, and painters Giovanni D'Agostino and Micaëla Henich. Raworth lives in Cambridge, England.

Lisa Robertson's poetry books include *XEclogue* (Tsunami, 1993), *Debbie: An Epic* (New Star, 1997), *The Weather* (New Star, 2001), and *Occasional Work and Seven Walks from the Office for Soft Architecture* (Clear Cut, 2003). A former member of the Kootenay School of Writing in Vancouver, Robertson now lives in Paris.

Juliana Spahr's books of poetry include *Response* (Sun and Moon, 1996), *Fuck You-Aloha-I Love You* (Wesleyan, 2001), and *The Connection of Everyone with Lungs* (California, 2005). She is also author of the critical study *Everybody's Autonomy: Connective Reading and Collective Identity* (Alabama, 2000) and co-editor of *Chain*. Spahr teaches English at Mills College and lives in Oakland.

Rod Smith is the author of several books of poetry including *In Memory of My Theories* (O, 1996), *Protective Immediacy* (Roof, 1999), *The Good House* (Spectacular Books, 2001), and *Music or Honesty* (Roof, 2003). Smith lives in Washington D.C., where he curates a reading series at Bridge Street Books and edits Aerial/Edge books.

Brian Kim Stefans is author of *Gulf* (Object, 1998), *Free Space Comics* (Roof, 1998), *A Poem of Attitudes* (self-published, 2000), *Angry Penguins* (Harry Tankoos, 2000), and the critical book *Fashionable Noise: On Digital Poetics* (Atelos, 2002). Stefans teaches at the Richard Stockton College of New Jersey.

Lynne Tillman's novels and short-story collections include *Haunted Houses* (Poseidon, 1987), *Motion Sickness* (Poseidon, 1991), *The Madame Realism Complex* (Semiotext(e), 1992), and *American Genius, A Comedy* (Soft Skull, 2006). Tillman lives in New York City and teaches English at SUNY Albany.

Edwin Torres' books of poetry include *Lung Poetry* (Sonico, 1994), *Fractured Humorous* (Subpress, 1999), and *The All-Union Day of the Shock Worker* (Roof, 2001). Torres has also published the CD *Holy Kid* (Kill Rock Stars, 1998). Torres now edits the e-poetry journal *POeP* and lives in New York City.

Cecilia Vicuña is an artist and writer from Chile who has exhibited her work internationally since the early 1970s. Her poetry has been widely anthologized. Vicuña's books of poetry include *Saborami* (Beau Geste, 1973), *Precario/Precarious* (Tanam, 1983), *PALABRARmas* (Ediciones El Imaginero, 1984), Word & Thread (Morning Star, 1996), and *QUIPOem* (Wesleyan, 1997). She lives in New York City.

Lewis Warsh's poetry books include *Hives* (United Artists, 1979) and *Methods of Birth Control* (Sun and Moon, 1983). He has also written two books of fiction, *Agnes & Sally* (Fiction Collective, 1984) and *Money Under the Table* (Trip Street, 1997). Warsh lives in New York City and teaches creative writing at Long Island University, Brooklyn.

Barrett Watten's poetry books include *Progress* (Roof, 1985), *Frame* (Sun and Moon, 1997), and *Bad History* (Atelos, 1998), as well as the critical books *Total Syntax* (Southern Illinois, 1985) and *The Constructivist Moment* (Wesleyan, 2003). Watten lives in Detroit, where he teaches literature and cultural studies at Wayne State University.

Marjorie Welish's books of poetry include *Handwritten* (Sun Press, 1979), *The Windows Flew Open* (Burning Deck, 1991), and *The Annotated "Here" and Selected Poems* (Coffee House, 2000). Her art criticism has been collected in *Signifying Art: Essays on Art After 1960* (Cambridge, 1999). Welish lives in New York City.

Kevin Young's poetry books are *Most Way Home* (William Morrow, 1995) and *To Repel Ghosts* (Zoland, 2001). His poems have been published in journals including *Callaloo, Hambone,* and *Grand Street*. He edited *Giant Steps: The New Generation of African American Writers* (Harper, 2000) and teaches at Indiana University.

CREDITS

Ammiel Alcalay: From *From the Warring Factions* (Beyond Baroque, 2002)

John Ashbery: "Alone, I" and "Intricate Fasting" from As *Umbrellas Follow Rain* (Qua Books, 2001). Copyright © 2001 by John Ashbery. All rights reserved. Used by permission of the author and Georges Borchardt, Inc.

Christian Bok: From *Eunoia* (Coach House, 2001)

Lee Ann Brown: "Vision Crown"; "Institutional Velvet"; "Ballad of Amiri B" from *The Sleep that Changed Everything* (Wesleyan, 2003)

Jeff Derksen: From *But Could I Make a Living From It* (Hole, 2000)

Marcella Durand: "Machine into Water 23" from *Western Capital Rhapsodies* (Faux, 2001)

Dan Farrell: From *The Inkblot Record* (Coach House, 2000)

Nada Gordon and Gary Sullivan: From *Swoon* (Granary, 2001)

Carla Harryman: "Expansion" from *The Words: After Carl Sandburg's Rootabaga Stories and Jean Paul Sartre* (O, 1999)

Susan Howe: "These Flames and Generosities of the Heart: Emily Dickinson and the Illogic of Sumptuary Values" from *The Birth-mark: unsettling the Wilderness in American Literary History* (Wesleyan University Press, 1993)

Rachel Levitsky: "Seasonal [Deleted]" and "Crises" from *Under the Sun* (Future Poem, 2003)

Ben Marcus: "The Name Machine" from *Notable American Women* (Vintage, 2002).

Emily McVarish: From *Was Here* (Granary, 2001)

Tom Raworth: "Intellectual Compost Four"; "Unable to Create Carrier"; "Rhodopsin Blues"; "No Music" from *Meadow* (Post Apollo, 1999)

Lynne Tillman: "Madame Realism Lies Here" from the anthology *Here Lies*, eds. David Gilbert and Karl Roeseler (Trip Street, 2001)

Barrett Watten: "The 1980s" from *Bad History* (Atelos, 1998)

Marjorie Welish: "Textile #6"; "Textile #7"; "Textile #10"; "Textile #13" from *Textile* (Equipage, 2000)

Kevin Young: "Gray" and "Heaven" from *To Repel Ghosts* (Zoland, 2001)

All texts included in this volume are reprinted by permission of the author except where noted otherwise.